OCCASIONAL PAPERS IN INTERNATIONAL AFFAIRS
Number 11
November 1965

PAN-AFRICANISM IN ACTION

An Account of the UAM

By Albert Tevoedjre

Published by the
Center for International Affairs
Harvard University

ABOUT THE AUTHOR

Albert Tevoedjre—born in Porto-Novo, Dahomey, in 1929, educated in Europe, and widely traveled in Africa, the United States, and the Soviet Union—is Coordinator of African Activities of the International Labour Office, a post he took up in 1965 after spending a year as a Fellow of the Center for International Affairs.

He holds a doctorate in economics and social science from the University of Fribourg (Switzerland) and degrees for advanced study in history and international relations from the University of Geneva and the University of Toulouse. During his student years, he edited the journal of the Fédération des Etudiants d'Afrique Noire en France.

Upon returning to Dahomey in 1959, Mr. Tevoedjre was elected by his colleagues Deputy Secretary-General of the Syndicat National des Enseignants and a member of the board of the Union Générale des Travailleurs du Dahomey. After the proclamation of independence in 1960, he became Minister of Information in Dahomey and soon after was named Secretary-General of the Union Africaine et Malgache (UAM), the supranational organization described in this paper.

Since leaving the UAM in 1963, he has taught at the African Institute at Geneva and at Georgetown University (Washington, D.C.). He is the author of *L'Afrique révoltée* (Paris, 1958), *La formation des cadres africains en vue de la croissance économique* (Paris, 1965), and *L'Afrique face aux problèmes du socialisme et de l'aide étrangère* (Bad Godesberg, 1965).

ACKNOWLEDGMENTS

In the life of every man a few places, a few dates stand out as turning points.

The period of my stay at Harvard, more specifically at the Center for International Affairs, constitutes for me one such decisive episode. I am happy that a publication, even a modest one, can mark this occurrence.

The encouragement, collaboration, and friendship of several members of the University community have been invaluable to me in my writing, and it is a very pleasant duty to acknowledge warmly my debt to them. I alone, however, must bear the responsibility for errors, oversights, and the opinions expressed here.

The warm interest of Professor Rupert Emerson, under whose direction I undertook this exposition of facts and ideas, as well as his profound knowledge of African problems and his frank criticism, provided a dependable touchstone for my study.

The foundations of this paper were laid in a seminar presided over by Professor Samuel Huntington. Among the participants in that seminar were: Ruth Schachter Morgenthau, Stanley Hoffmann, Benjamin Brown, O. Rudolph Aggrey, Willard Johnson, Robert Rotberg, Joseph Nye, Kwamena Bentsi-Enchill, Godfried van Benthem van den Bergh, Karl Kaiser, and ten of the Center's Fellows from America, Europe, and Asia. Each of them, as friend and colleague, freely expressed to me his point of view. I hope this paper reflects as much as possible the light their good will cast on my subject.

But I must express my gratitude in particular to those who agreed to collaborate with me during the summer of 1965. First, I owe thanks to Miss Lois Pattison, tutor in history and literature at Harvard, who translated the greater part of this text from a prolix French style into serviceable English, while leaving my ideas intact. I also cordially thank Robert Erwin, Editor of Publications at the Center, who helped to make the text more orderly. And I especially want to express my gratitude to my friend Joseph Nye, who acted as "technical advisor" and gave generously of his time to help me structure this work. I have drawn much benefit from his rare understanding of the problems facing regional and international organizations, as well as from his special concern with the relations between the states of East Africa.

But I would never have been able to thank all these friends and colleagues, I could not have written this work, if I had not enjoyed the constant and personal attention of Professor Robert Bowie, Director of the Center, and of Dr. Benjamin Brown, Advisor to the Fellows of the Center—and if my wife and my children had not accepted my numerous absences as part of the price of our mutual determination to contribute to the full participation of a mature Africa in the affairs of a difficult world.

A. TEVOEDJRE

Oberlin, Ohio
August 8, 1965

CONTENTS

MEMBERS OF THE UAM

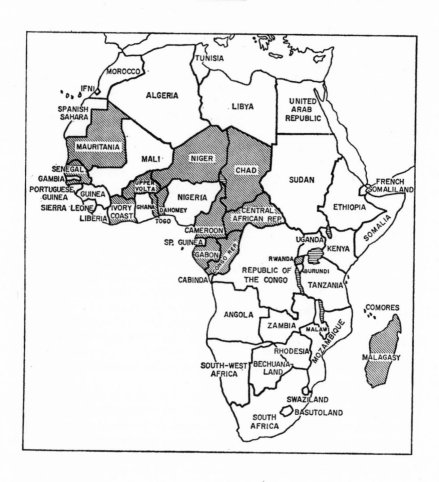

I

Introduction

Proclamations of faith in Pan-Africanism or African unity are not new. They have been numerous and fervid.

The early Pan-African movements originated in the Western Hemisphere, essentially as a protest against racism. This phase reached its peak in the 1920's with the growth of Garveyism in the United States. Liberia and Sierra Leone were the earliest fruits of Pan-Africanism. As carefully analyzed by Immanuel Wallerstein and other writers, the Fifth Pan-African Conference, organized by the American Negro W.E.B. Du Bois in 1945 and attended by George Padmore, Kwame Nkrumah, and Jomo Kenyatta (among others), marked a change. Henceforth Pan-Africanism became a rallying point for African forces struggling for national independence. Then, when independence was achieved but at the cost of splintering Africa into a host of states—sovereignty without unity—the focus of Pan-Africanism shifted again. Today it stands for reorganizing the continent along supranational lines.

At least four important current approaches to Pan-Africanism can be distinguished. They are the rigorous federalist approach of Nkrumah, the confederalist idea of Senghor, the policy of coordination advocated by Houphouet-Boigny, and the Arab-Islamic plan attributed to Nasser.

President Nkrumah of Ghana, the spiritual heir of Du Bois and Marcus Garvey, is among those who think that African unity must mean, with no ambiguity, a United States of Africa. In his writings, his domestic speeches, and his addresses at international conferences he has repeated two ideas emphatically: that African countries cannot escape from poverty unless they combine their resources; that a United States of Africa, like the Soviet Union and the United States of America, could become a great power.

President Leopold Sédar Senghor of Senegal developed his approach in response to the *loi-cadre* of 1957, which compartmentalized the French African territories. It was he who hit on the term "balkanization" for the way in which formerly associated colonies were being brought to autonomy. Senghor and Modibo Keita, President of

[1]

the Republic of Mali, were soon promoting a limited regional grouping based on historical and cultural ties. At Dakar in 1959, Senegal, the Sudan, Dahomey, and Upper Volta formed the Federation of Mali, but this soon collapsed when Dahomey withdrew under pressure from the Ivory Coast and President Maurice Yameogo of Upper Volta claimed that he had not "really" sworn allegiance to Mali. Subsequently, while adapting his ideas to new circumstances, Senghor has continued to advocate regional confederations.

President Felix Houphouet-Boigny of the Ivory Coast favors the gradual growth of supranational ties from the cooperation of sovereign states in their respective immediate interests. At Addis Ababa he spoke of "transitory forms of association in order to arrive at unity," knowing that his Conseil de l'Entente—consisting of the Ivory Coast, Upper Volta, Niger, and Dahomey and formed to counteract the Mali Federation—has survived when more ambitious organizations have not. Financial, legal, military, and diplomatic coordination binds the Entente countries, limited and not always unanimous but constant.

With President Nasser of the UAR (United Arab Republic), a very special version of Pan-Africanism is preached because of obvious differences between the Arabs and their southern neighbors. These differences notwithstanding, approximately 90 million Muslims are now to be found in Africa, and it is possible that by 1980 half the population of the continent will be Muslim. Moreover, though a religious faith expressed in a common language may be the only solid tie between Muslims, there are reciprocal influences between Pan-African and Pan-Arab aspirations, and President Nasser is ideally poised at the cross-roads. Cairo, the home of various Afro-Asian organizations since 1957, has become a refuge for nationalists, opposition leaders, and students from all over Africa. Radio Cairo broadcasts in 22 languages, including several African dialects. After first aligning with the Casablanca Group, Nasser put the UAR on good terms with Guinea and Cameroon and then at Addis Ababa ingratiated himself with all African countries. One might assume that he would favor regional groupings which would allow him to reconcile his major spheres of interest.

The history of Pan-Africanism sketched above stresses ideas and intentions. Impersonal factors working for and against African unity must also be mentioned. And, most important, the political, economic, and cultural substance of an actual supranational African organization remains to be described.

Centrifugal forces are strong in Africa. If Pan-Africanism has become a glorious myth and an intellectual imperative, it is still true that daily life in the villages is marked by traditional hatreds, family and tribal feuds, mutual distrust. The continent itself, with its cortege of 36 independent states and a sprinkling of dependent territories, is fragmented like a broken mirror. Africa will never constitute an optimum zone of development so long as it remains, in the words of Jean-Paul Sartre, "a land compartmentalized, bristling with barriers, partitions, chicanery, where every man has a bone to pick with his neighbor."[1] Yet the high costs of fragmentation may be viewed as an inducement to keep on seeking unity. They complement the positive arguments for integration.

Practical problems of unity—written about from personal experience and in terms of particular successes and failures—are the subject of this paper. The case dealt with is that of the former territories of French West Africa, French Equatorial Africa, and Madagascar. In 1960, twelve (later fourteen) states from these areas formed the Union Africaine et Malgache, sometimes identified in English as the African and Malagasy Union and commonly referred to as the UAM. I was Secretary-General of the UAM, which is now officially dissolved but whose former member states still acknowledge some ties and engage in loose forms of cooperation.

The UAM's efforts toward economic, technical, and cultural progress illustrate both the negative and positive inducements to greater African unity. Problems of "balkanization" and "vassalization" —the topic of the next section—were and are faced not only by the French-speaking countries but in some form by nearly all developing nations.

BALKANIZATION AND VASSALIZATION

The conditions under which independence was accorded to the French-speaking African states are well known.[2] As long as the colonial territories had to be governed, they were grouped together. This grouping facilitated administration and organized the economy to the benefit of the colonial power.

But, from the moment that the system of direct administration was to break up, it appeared necessary to find some fashion of dividing up the old empire in order to keep it more effectively under thumb. Grouped together, the former colonies would be a partner; divided, they would form a mosaic of minuscule dependent states and remain subject to the metropolitan power. In the *loi-cadre*, France chose to break apart the old grouping so as to leave the French government in a position to wield the arm of flattery and of economic differentiation among the small independent states thus constituted.

---

[1]Sartre, "Les Grenouilles qui demandent un roi," *Situations V* (Paris: Gallimard, 1964), 113.

[2]See Ruth Schachter Morgenthau, *Political Parties in French-speaking West Africa* (London: Oxford University Press, 1964); W. Foltz, *From French West Africa to the Mali Federation* (New Haven: Yale University Press, 1965).

No one believes in the possibility of a dialogue between David and Goliath, between the United States and Costa Rica. What then can be said of France and Upper Volta? The Prefect of the Bouches du Rhone and even the Prefect of the Lot govern interests greater than the President of the Republic of Chad or of Togo.

As Joseph Kizerbo pertinently asks:

> How can such a state negotiate on an equal footing with an ex-metropole, which helped to install it politically, which provides it with all its currency for imports, which makes up the chronic deficits in its operating budget, and which sometimes even maintains on the territory of its protégé military forces ten times superior in number to the local national troops?[3]

In the words of François Perroux:

> *Economically apparent* nations and *economically real* nations converse, while brandishing the flag of sovereignty.[4]

Because of several conditions, minuscule states cannot help lending themselves easily to a new domination. First, the multiplicity of governments demands a substantial number of technical civil servants, who are in short supply in Africa. The result is an influx of technical-assistance personnel, who then control the apparatus of the state for a prolonged period of time. Second, the weakness of the budgets of the micro-states favors the "sugar-cube policy," by which industrial states grant aid to preserve lucrative markets. Third, balkanization results in frontier disputes and petty rivalry which benefits the former metropole and promotes vassalization.

A federal government installed in Dakar, Abidjan, or Brazzaville would have required fewer foreign civil servants than are necessary in the maintenance of eight independent states. In a federal government, for instance, a single Ministry of Foreign Affairs would have been sufficient. Today they are eight, each with its own cabinet, central services, and embassies. It is evident that the recruitment of men to fill all these positions is not easy in Chad, Niger, or Upper Volta. Even the more fortunate countries like Dahomey, the Ivory Coast, Cameroon, or Madagascar are not untroubled by some shortages and some blatant failures. It is not sufficient to hold a law degree, a *Baccalaureate*, a *brevet élémentaire*, or a degree from the Institut des Hautes Études d'Outre-Mer to direct the Treasury, the Ministry of the Interior, or the National Planning Board competently.

The key positions in the administration of a country are often found in: the general secretariat of the President and general secre-

---

[3]Kizerbo, addressing the Conference Rencontres Internationales de Geneve (September, 1963).

[4]Perroux, *L'économie des jeunes nations* (Paris: Presses Universitaires de France, 1962), p. 11.

tariat of the government; the general staff of the army and office of security; the information service; the planning office; the central office and major overseas posts of the foreign-affairs ministry; and the central offices of economic affairs. In 1960-62, ten out of twelve French-speaking African states entrusted the general secretariat of their governments to French nationals. In Dahomey, two former French administrators were still entrusted with a prefecture. In all twelve states, the Office of Coded Telegrams was managed by a former French administrator. In the Congo-Brazzaville, then under President Fulbert Youlou, nine key positions were filled by former French colonial officials.

What we point out was not true merely of French-speaking states but was only more extreme there. After having tried several experiments himself, President Nkrumah affirms in his autobiography:

> It has always been my conviction that after any political revolution, non-violent or violent, the new government should immediately, on coming into power, clear out from the civil service all its old leaders. My own experience taught me that by failing to do so, a revolutionary government risks its own destruction.[5]

If such is the fate of a so-called revolutionary government, what of states that became independent merely by "transfer of legal competence"?

The recent plots in numerous African states have shed light on the possible complicity of some former metropoles in preparing the removal of their partners of yesterday and today. The thinkers of the sixteenth century were not wrong:

> They have the power to depose a king, who also
> have the power to create one.

Economic Control—The "Sugar-Cube Policy"

If it is true that one goal of any colonizing power is to find clients for its production, then we can easily understand the system perfected for this purpose over the years. Because of financial difficulties and for reasons inherent in the very principles of the colonial regime, a colonized territory can import certain quantities of merchandise only thanks to the loans furnished by the former metropoles or by richer countries. These loans or facilities can take a particular form: that of imperial preferences for the export of tropical produce, permitting the "beneficiary" countries to have the material wherewithal to purchase merchandise that they could not otherwise acquire.

---

[5] *Ghana: The Autobiography of Kwame Nkrumah* (Edinburgh: Nelson, 1959), p. 122.

Once the system is installed and has passed traditionally into the customs of the country, it is difficult to bring about a change, even after independence. The former colonial monopolies preserve their outlets and maintain their privileges; the countries subject to this form of aid are constantly tied to it and often cannot envisage a way to cut the Gordian knot.

In buying African cotton at a price above the world price in order to meet 15 to 20 per cent of its needs, France not only realizes an economy in currency outflows for her foreign trade but also makes it possible for the Africans whom she aids in this way to be able to purchase in France at relatively high prices merchandise which they would not be in a position to acquire without this particular system of exchange. Thus Dahomey, for instance, purchases three-fourths ad valorem of its merchandise within the Franc Zone, and it sends on the average 80 per cent of its exports to France. Even when the world market for raw materials is at its worst, Dahomey is sustained by France, which purchases some products at a price higher than the world level. But this is on the condition that the benefit thus realized will be spent on imports that favor French industry. The figures speak for themselves. Dahomey sold to France 68,131 tons of products for a value of 2,581,809,000 francs CFA in 1961; but it purchased 76,921 tons of merchandise for a value of 3,679,271,000 francs CFA.[6] Customs receipts and taxes somewhat compensate for the disparity, but the deficit becomes a daily burden. Then France tries to come to the rescue and agrees to balance the administrative budget. She has already provided more than 3 billion francs CFA to the Dahomey government to soak up the budgetary deficit between 1960, the year of national independence, and 1963. If this support were suddenly removed, Dahomey would run the risk of catastrophe, of asphyxiation.

This system resembles a rope thrown to an alpinist, clinging to a cliff and exhausted. The rope thrown to him saves him from immediate death, but so long as he remains hanging in the air, he is at the mercy of the person holding the rope. That is precisely the case of the client-state chained to its protector's market, so that, prevented from developing its commerce with other states, its situation grows worse. Dependence becomes automatic as the two economies are knit together. The method is like a Pavlovian technique which might be called "the sugar-cube policy." The powerful state informs a weak government in difficulty that it is ready to come to its aid to the tune of several billions. The client-state then becomes hypnotized by the lure of the promised billions, in much the same way as an animal in the laboratory might be by the sugar cube. But the client-state is only given sufficient time to nibble a corner off the sugar cube, so that

---

[6]Cf. *Dahomey: Naissance d'une nation* (Paris, 1963).

its hunger is not satisfied. Most aid is indeed extended for a short term: one month, two months, a year at the maximum, and it is always insufficient to cover entirely the needs of the period concerned. The beggar is thus perpetually uncertain. Pulled into an almost scientifically refined combination, he is unceasingly obliged to solicit new credit and to be careful of any "imprudence" likely to annoy his protector—notably in economic, political, and diplomatic affairs. The result is diplomatic bondage.

For example, several of the French-speaking African states were very timid about offending France during the Algerian conflict. When I was Minister of Information in Dahomey, I happened to take to task on a radio broadcast a French lawyer who, in defending a Dahomey citizen during a political trial, had maintained, contrary to the facts, that his client had been brutally mistreated. He protested notably against barbarous methods unworthy of a civilized people. In my broadcast speech, I stated that those who had tortured Djamilla Bouhired and Henri Alleg in Algeria hardly had the right to preach to Dahomey, especially when their evidence was supported by lies to boot. This statement stirred up a certain commotion. The French Ambassador protested officially to the President of the Republic of Dahomey and telegraphed to alert his government, all of which of course placed me in a rather uncomfortable position. Despite the fact that I pointed out to the Cabinet members that it was abnormal and even inadmissible that a French lawyer, and in the bargain a deputy of the French government majority (the issue concerned Maître Pasquini, a UNR deputy), should plead in court against the Dahomey government, while it would be inconceivable that a lawyer from Dahomey, under similar conditions, should ever plead in favor of an accused OAS prisoner in Paris, I was constrained to go "explain" my statement to His Excellency, the French Ambassador.

Another example is a statement made by a certain important Dahomean government official upon his return from a state visit to Eastern Europe. Finding this statement too flattering to the Soviet Union and likely to displease the government of the former metropole, the head of government took it upon himself to prohibit the circulation of the statement, after having called the ambassador of the protecting power to listen to the recording.

SIZE AND TECHNIQUES

It may be that the daily penalties of balkanization will provide the most impetus for African cooperation. Nevertheless, there is more to Pan-Africanism than merely trying to make a bad situation more bearable. As is evident in the case of the United States, the Soviet Union, Communist China, and the steadily growing European union,

[7]

positive benefits flow from massing manpower, resources, and political direction. Africans are aware of this, and every day that passes brings with it a greater belief in the strength to be gained from an organized union. As President Senghor, looking beyond the UAM, has said, "The goal remains to construct together the entire continent."[7]

Nor are African leaders unaware of what might be called the technical dynamics of integration. The analysis by Louis Armand, one of the greatest French technocrats, demonstrating the necessity of European union, has been studied, for example, with a view to its applicability in Africa. According to Armand, the modern world is governed by two principles. The first is that of *size* or dimension. The second is that of *acceleration* in the evolution of *techniques*. He finds that modern techniques impose a certain dimension and that they evolve rapidly. In addition, they call for more and more costly equipment, which in turn grows obsolete with increasing rapidity. Technical imperatives thus lead inevitably to the conception of large-scale units.

This analysis applies just as well to Africa today. The underdevelopment of the continent is a global phenomenon requiring global solutions integrated in intense international cooperation.

How can these solutions be achieved? How can economically apparent nations be transformed into economically real nations? The answer is perhaps to be found in the new principle of international existence set forth by François Perroux as "the right of peoples to multinational poles of development." "It is by the solidarity of the *plurinational* infrastructure" and "new forms of production and exchange that cultural communities will find their material foundations and will draw forth the immense resources necessary to the formation of the inspirers, the animators, and the monitors of the collective creation."[8]

Once the principles of the collective creation are recognized, they must be put to the test through both the majesty of ideas and the pragmatism of daily life. I think that the well-known difficulties of Africa's independent states can be solved by transcending the narrow framework of balkanized sovereignties. This conviction is not universally shared, and by undertaking this study I hope to clarify what to many of us seems to be the most promising policy for Africa. It is not, however, the purely political aspect of Pan-Africanism that concerns me here. I should also like to contribute to the studies currently in process in universities among specialists in problems of regional integration and international organizations. The example of the UAM, whose structure and evolution are presented here, will perhaps serve

---

[7]L. S. Senghor, opening address at the Bangui Conference of the UAM (March, 1962).

[8]Perroux, *L'économie des jeunes nations*, pp. 226–27.

to reinforce or to refine certain concepts and analyses developed in the work of such scholars as Ernst Haas.

Having noted some of the difficulties and incentives involved in the creation and administration of regional organizations—among states hesitating to take the final step to fusion, while desiring to maintain ties in a flexible cooperation often of limited effectiveness—we can now pass on directly to the Union Africaine et Malgache.

II

The Success and Failure of the UAM

Establishment

Three major series of events led to the formation of the UAM.

First, there were the compromises and efforts toward unity born of the dismemberment of the former French federations of the AOF (Afrique Occidentale Française) and AEF (Afrique Equatoriale Française). When the attempt to form a federal executive and to maintain in other forms the councils of the AOF and AEF ended in failure, new groups based on the inclinations and interests of the various statesmen were formed: the Federation of Mali, the Conseil de l'Entente, the Union of the Central African Republics (URAC), the Union Douanière Equatoriale (UDE).

The dissolution of the Federation of Mali and the admission of Bamako to the Ghana-Guinea group placed Senegal in a position of isolation vis-à-vis the Ivory Coast, its major rival. Senegalese leaders therefore paved the way for a rapprochement with Abidjan in the framework of a "club" enlarged to include French-speaking states, most of whose leaders had attended similar schools and often the same school (William Ponty), belonged to similar or identical political parties (Houphouet-Boigny's Rassemblement Démocratique Africain, Senghor's Indépendants d'Outre-Mer and Convention Africaine), and had almost all been members of the French Parliamentary Assemblies, where they had come to know and respect one another. After the colonies were given autonomy and independence, these leaders missed the forum provided by the Palais Bourbon or the councils of the AOF and AEF, where they had met together regularly. Several of them, without admitting it, found in the UAM this "club" that they thought back to nostalgically.

During the month of July, 1960, Mamadou Dia, then Prime Minister of Senegal, went to Cotonou to see President Houphouet-Boigny of the Ivory Coast, who was in Dahomey attempting to arbitrate a local conflict between his political partners, Justin Ahomadegbé and Hubert Maga. It was at Cotonou, during the consultations between Houphouet-Boigny and Mamadou Dia, that the idea of regrouping the

[10]

French-speaking African states was born, thus permitting Senegal to escape the isolation threatened by the collapse of the Mali Federation. At a preliminary conference at Abidjan on October 26, 1960, the heads of the French-speaking states agreed to meet periodically and to take a common stand on international questions.

The second set of events bearing on the formation of the UAM had to do with the position of France in 1960. The worst hour of the Algerian War was at hand. Negotiations were bogged down. Several Afro-Asian, Socialist, and even Western states seriously contemplated a United Nations intervention. The De Gaulle government was resolutely hostile to such a solution.

Whether or not the idea was entirely their own, Houphouet-Boigny, Senghor, and their friends wanted to avoid a recourse to the UN. They united in the Brazzaville Group, which then represented 11 per cent of the votes in the United Nations, and their action was successful in blocking a UN intervention in the Algerian affair.

Third, the UAM to some extent owed its existence and development to the Congo crisis, over which African states were and still remain sharply divided. It was above all at the Brazzaville Conference of December 19, 1960, that the UAM became a reality.[1] Fulbert Youlou, then President of the former French Congo and dreaming of a great and united Congo, opened the assembly "in the name of all the Congolese." Aside from the Congolese question, which occupied half of the three-day conference but whose solution wasn't really even begun at Brazzaville, the conference strove to define a policy of cooperation in the diplomatic, military, economic, and cultural realms. It was decided that experts should meet at Dakar to study practical formulas of cooperation, including a permanent framework for development of the African economy, and that the results of these studies would then be presented at the next summit conference.

The participants at Brazzaville strongly emphasized that if the realization of these objectives necessitated a regional organization, this organization would have to respect the political individuality of the member states, *whose sovereignty was in no way to be called into question.* In matters of diplomacy, the Brazzaville Conference considered that "the fundamental principle was the persistent search for peace." In all international conflicts it was decided that the policy would be "not to side with the opponents, but rather to conciliate them; not to propose just any compromise, but rather to invite the

---

[1]Represented at the Brazzaville Conference were the twelve states which founded the UAM, and Congo-Leopoldville attended as an observer. This was at the time of the first Congolese crisis. Kasavubu, Tshombe, and Mobutu came to Brazzaville, but Lumumba was already in prison. See below, p. 67, for a complete list of UAM conferences.

opponents to enter into the kind of dialogue out of which can come a solution leading to peace and international cooperation."

The states of the Brazzaville Group did not heartily endorse Patrice Lumumba and his ideas. And while they did for the most part display strong reservations about the secession of Katanga Province, none adopted a militant position against Moise Tshombe. They even went so far as to denounce the attitude of those African states favoring the followers of Lumumba. At the Brazzaville Conference they adopted a resolution stating: "The [undersigned] African and Malagasy States pay tribute to the effort undertaken by the United Nations to save the Congo-Leopoldville from chaos and anarchy. . . ." *"Unfortunately, rival blocs have attempted and are still attempting to recolonize the Congo-Leopoldville, either directly or indirectly through the agency of certain Afro-Asian States."*

The allusion to the Ghana, Guinea, Mali, UAR group was clear. These states were bound to react.

The Brazzaville Resolution was dated December 19, 1960. On January 3, 1961, King Mohammed V of Morocco called a conference in Casablanca. This conference was a violent response to the Brazzaville Conference. To begin with, the Brazzaville Group had supported down the line the position of Mauritania, which Morocco hoped to annex. This was reason in itself for Rabat's hostile feeling. Then, the steps taken by the pro-Lumumba African states required a certain coordination. Finally, the Algerian problem was not analyzed in the same light by Presidents Houphouet-Boigny and Senghor, on the one hand, and President Sékou Touré of Guinea and President Nasser, on the other.

At the Casablanca Conference, Morocco, Ghana, Guinea, Mali, the UAR, and the Algerian Provisional Government formed the Casablanca Group, pro-Lumumba, pro-GPRA (Algerian Provisional Government), violently anti-Tshombe, and proclaiming the strictest non-alignment with the superpowers.

In order to reconcile the two rival blocs (Brazzaville and Casablanca), Senegal, Togo, the Ivory Coast, Nigeria, and Liberia took the initiative in calling a conference to be held in Monrovia on May 8, 1961. The states of the Casablanca Group boycotted this meeting.[2]

---

[2]It seems that Mali and Guinea were under pressure from Ghana and the UAR to abstain from the Monrovia Conference. This fact sheds light on the opening statement of President Tubman:

"I have observed that there seems to be three schools of thought on this subject [of leadership]. There are those who feel that Liberia should assume leadership based on the fact that she is the oldest African Republic and is riper in political experience; but it will require more than age and political experience to assume leadership of Africa. There are others who assume that Ghana should assume that role because she is physically more developed and embraces larger territories. It will require more than development and larger territory to assume

[12]

It was attended by the twelve Brazzaville states plus Liberia, Nigeria, Somalia, Sierra Leone, Togo, Ethiopia, and Libya.[3]

Thus the Monrovia Group came into being, and for two years it was to be a sort of Brazzaville Group enlarged to include the English-speaking countries, although the latter harbored great reservations concerning their French-speaking colleagues, whom they accused of excessive fidelity to Paris. It was precisely the characteristics peculiar to the French-speaking countries that led them to preserve their separate identity in the UAM in addition to joining in the formation of the Monrovia Group.

The French-speaking countries convened a second time at Yaoundé, March 26–28, 1961, where they adopted resolutions presented by the experts who had met at Dakar, and they agreed to the creation of an Organisation Africaine et Malgache de Coopération Économique (OAMCE). President Ahmadou Ahidjo of the Federal Republic of Cameroon told his colleagues, "We believe that the classical forms of colonialism have been decisively left behind. We are not falling back into the past by meditating on our hatreds and disappointments; we are resolved to turn to the present realities, in order to be able to look towards the future, free from all resentment and all passion."

By the third conference, at Tananarive in September, 1961, the UAM was functioning as a regional organization equipped with the administrative structures and techniques which made it one of the most important organs of solidarity on the continent of Africa. President Philibert Tsiranana of Malagasy declared in his opening address:

> We former colonies, now liberated, have felt the need to regroup ourselves even more than was possible in the past. Our needs were the same, our situation similar. We had every reason to defend our common interests. Now, the entire world recognizes us as a political and economic reality. Our firm determination to continue in harmonizing our diplomacy will certainly bring us the consideration and esteem of the majority. We have already proven that our political ties did not blind us, however delicate the decisions we have had to make. . . .[4]

The Monrovia Group to which the UAM members belonged con-

---

leadership of Africa. And there are yet those who opine that Egypt with its rich traditions dating back to the remotest antiquity should do so. It will require more than rich traditions of antiquity. It will require, in my opinion, the aggregate of the best that is in all compounded in such a manner as to represent the divisibility of Africa indivisible."

[3]Libya had been represented at the Casablanca Conference in January. It chose soon after the conference to assume a certain distance in its relations with the Casablanca powers and so joined the Monrovia Group.

[4]This was an allusion to the Algerian War and to the African negotiations carried on with General de Gaulle in search of a peaceful settlement.

tinued to exist along fairly similar political lines. This coalition as a whole found itself working at cross-purposes with the Casablanca Group, which declared itself militant, revolutionary, and socialist. The creation of the Organization of African Unity (OAU) at Addis Ababa in May, 1963, was intended, in theory, to mark the end of all these rival unions.

Operations

It is unfortunate that present-day Africa should be so jostled by time, because time must be taken into consideration before an achievement is judged. Unfortunately, many of the accomplishments of the UAM remained in the stage of projects, sometimes highly advanced but rarely mature.

To begin with, the UAM realized the necessity of having regulative principles and provided itself with constitutional documents: the UAM Charter, the OAMCE Pact, the UAMD Pact (defense), the UAMPT Pact (postal and telecommunications), and the Air Afrique Pact (joint airline).

But it was not enough to create these organizational structures on paper. It was also necessary to bring them to life, by choosing men to run them and appropriating sufficient funds.

Praiseworthy efforts were made. Certain states, for example, consented to place key officials at the disposal of the UAM. If the budgets were not overflowing with funds, at least they were sufficient for the cost of material maintenance, the needs of the officials, and for the realization of the specific goals set by the organization.

The total budget was 300 million francs CFA, and, remarkably, all states paid their quota regularly; some even paid more than was required. This must be a rather rare occurrence in the history of international organizations, and it symbolizes the exceptional will to succeed which was one of the prime forces of the UAM. In the same light it is worth pointing out that contrary to what could be observed in the Casablanca Group, the heads of state of the UAM met often and on the scheduled dates. At Tananarive, ten out of twelve heads of state were present, and the other two were represented by trusted ministers. At Bangui also, ten heads of state attended; at Libreville all twelve were present; and eleven came to Ouagadougou.

At the initial conferences, possible forms of cooperation were discussed. For example, the former federations of the AOF and the AEF had allowed a Senegalese to be at home in Upper Volta and a native of Upper Volta to be perfectly at ease in Dahomey. But the centrifugal sovereignties of micro-nationalism menaced this freedom of movement. In an attempt to forestall the problems of balkanization the UAM created a Convention d'Établissement, "facilitating the exchange and circulation of persons between states."

[14]

A similar problem arose with regard to the tenure of civil servants. Because of the unevenness of education under colonial rule, Dahomean officials, for example, were numerous throughout French Africa. Even after independence various members of intermediate staffs serving in states from which they did not originally come remained indispensable. In order to deal with this problem, the heads of state decided to set up a Convention de Coopération Technique ("Pact for Technical Cooperation") allowing for the provision of officials. This was a complement to the Convention d'Établissement and constituted another way of counteracting the phenomenon of balkanization.

By the mere fact of its existence, the UAM was called upon to play a role in the anti-colonial struggle, the movement for Pan-African unity, and the mediation of particular crises such as those concerning Togo, Congo-Leopoldville, and Gabon's dispute with Congo-Brazzaville. On all of these problems, the UAM strove to maintain a common front. Two results were the membership of Rwanda and a very close association with Congo-Leopoldville.

On an international scale, following the Bangui Conference (March, 1962), the UAM heads of state were concerned with the coordination of diplomatic representation in order to avoid wasting manpower and money. The idea of common embassies was proposed, but it met with hesitations and even a certain degree of hostility. Instead emphasis was put on coordination and general problems. For instance, the UAM was totally unrepresented in Scandinavia, the majority of Asian countries, Central America, South America, Australia, and Eastern Europe. Thus the Secretariat prepared a report urging additional contacts:

> It is perhaps worth pointing out that, outside of the UAM states, several other African governments have entered into diplomatic relations with the Soviet Union. Furthermore, France, the United States, the Federal Republic of Germany, and Italy (home of the Vatican, as some have observed, not without malice) have all tried, in their own best interests and despite the enmity (of which we are aware) and the ideological attitude often expressed in public, to solve the problem posed by the presence in the world of over a billion people living in socialist countries and playing a role recognized by all, in the areas of economics and international politics. . . . At any rate, the world being what it is, and universal cooperation as well as non-alignment being our principle of foreign policy, it is important for us to analyze the problem in the best interests of the African and Malagasy Union—that is, in terms of its effectiveness and influence in Africa and in the world.

After discussing this report, the heads of state at the conference would go no farther than to say in very general terms that the UAM objective should be to make its presence universally felt and to work together on all questions of world politics.

[15]

An example of a case in which the UAM had the opportunity of putting this principle into practice was the New Guinea question. Indeed, when New Guinea (West Irian), the object of a dispute between Indonesia and the Netherlands, was presented as a problem to the United Nations, the UAM states were practically the only ones to insist that the right of self-determination be completely safeguarded and that, therefore, the Papuans be allowed the choice of joining or not joining Indonesia. But the Indonesian point of view prevailed, which meant the outright annexation of West Irian.

Action is not necessarily difficult when it is only a question of issuing administrative regulations, entering into negotiatons, or helping to calm a crisis. Such is not the case with economic questions. In this area the UAM needed more time and patience. The crucial problem was the persistence of the colonial economic situation caused by the excessive centralization of the economy of the Franc Zone. This made it difficult for the African countries to start producing for domestic consumption while importing as little as possible and exporting as much as possible.

In the course of many conferences, reports were presented by the OAMCE on the control of insurance, customs regulations, industrial property, and taxation, on a potential Union of African and Malagasy Development Banks, and on the eventual creation of a shipping company. In this matter, however, one must sympathize with President Yameogo, who in February, 1962, complained:

> The Government of Upper Volta is becoming more and more preoccupied with the very high number of ministerial and specialist conferences in which our government has to be represented. To the ministerial conferences, whether belonging directly to the activity of the UAM or whether belonging to the activity of the specialized secretariats, are added the meeting of the technical committees and committees created *ad hoc* as needs arise. These increases are costly and make it more difficult for the heads of ministerial departments to accomplish the duties for which they are held responsible in their respective governments.

If the economic efforts of the UAM were fraught with difficulties, encouraging results have nevertheless been obtained in closely related areas. Both Air Afrique and the union for postal service and telecommunications were highly successful.[5] In 1962, Air Afrique flew 10 million kilometers and 30,000 flight hours and carried 287,000 passengers and 15,000 tons of freight. This made it first in Africa in terms of kilometer-tons of freight transport and third in the world in the consumption coefficient of available tonnage.

The UAMPT was important because it meant that Paris was no

---

[5]Air Afrique does not serve Malagasy, which benefits from the services of a special company: Mad-Air.

longer the center of telecommunications for the states of the UAM. It used to be necessary to connect through Paris in order to telephone from Dakar to Tananarive. The UAMPT soon succeeded in freeing the African states from this costly, inconvenient, and politically embarrassing procedure. Among the numerous lines opened were: Dakar-Brazzaville; Dakar-Tananarive; Brazzaville-Tananarive; Brazzaville-Ouagadougou; and Douala-Tananarive.

These successes partly explain Rwanda's decision to apply for UAM membership and the interest shown by Congo-Leopoldville and Burundi.[6] A new slogan was even born out of this growth of the UAM—the idea of "borderless UAM."

The UAM could have emerged as the dominating force at the 1963 Addis Ababa Conference if it had known how to take advantage of its innate powers and of special factors like the Ivory Coast's ties with Guinea and Mali, Cameroon's sympathies with Egypt, and the exceptional geographic location of Dahomey in relation to Ghana, Togo, and Nigeria. This organization might have been destined for a great future, but a number of problems remained unsolved.

Lack of mutual trust was without a doubt the gravest of the UAM's shortcomings.[7] But other factors also hurt the prestige and effectiveness of the organization. There were conflicts among the Secretaries-General of the various agencies. While it was always affirmed that the UAM was a great single entity coordinating many technical structures to a common end, at the same time a veritable anarchy was allowed to exist in the administration. President Leon Mba of Gabon, acting President of the UAM, stated in a letter addressed to all the heads of state: "In my opinion it is abnormal, in an Organization as limited as ours, to have four Secretaries-General who all declare themselves equal, sovereign, independent." As each Secretariat tried to prove its own efficiency, the various governments found themselves submerged by conferences and documents. These conferences were not only numerous, but they were also sometimes uselessly overburdened and expensive. At Ouagadougou, for example, the daily agenda included over a hundred items, and the evenings were filled with folkloric manifestations which attracted a certain category of persons for whom these conferences were a gift from heaven. Such festivals became more and more expensive. The Bangui Conference (March, 1962) cost over 50 million francs CFA; Libreville (September,

---

[6]In 1962 and 1963 Congo-Leopoldville was considered an associate member of the UAM. Burundi sent observers to the Conferences of Libreville and Ouagadougou.

[7]For the historical background, refer to the quarrels between the territorialists and the federalists at the time of the *loi-cadre*, described in Morgenthau, *Political Parties of French-speaking West Africa*, and Foltz, *From French West Africa to the Mali Federation*.

1962) over 80 million; and Ouagadougou (March, 1963) over 100 million. Delegates, never fewer than 200, were lodged and fed by the particular state which was sponsoring the conference. If the results had justified all these expenses, there would have been cause for satisfaction. But the fact is that they did not.

The prime example of a non-functioning structure was the UAMD, which was supposed to combat subversion and coordinate resources to resist possible attack. The military means available in 1962 were: 3 battalion command units, 2 paratrooper companies, 11 companies with transport, and 4 transport units—a total of about 3,000 men. One might doubt whether 3,000 men, unaided from outside and using possibly defective infantry weapons, would have been able to intervene with any measure of success, particularly since they remained dispersed in the separate states.

The administration of the UAM was constantly disturbed by changes in personnel. Within a space of two years, the Secretariat in Cotonou was headed by four different men. This was owing to a kind of nationalization of the Secretariat-General carried out by President Hubert Maga of Dahomey, who was not able to get used to the idea of the non-nationalistic role of the UAM Secretary-General. In addition, within the member states, approximately two-thirds of the Ministers of Foreign Affairs were changed during an 18-month period; all the Ministers of Information were replaced, and cabinet reshuffling also affected other departments. Furthermore, certain spectacular dismissals did not enhance the prestige and the influence of the group.

The instability associated with these changes resulted in several abandoned plans, including one for an Institute for the Education of African Administrative Staffs, whose establishment had been prepared at Cotonou. The Carnegie Fund and the International Labour Office had concluded an agreement with the UAM for the creation of this center, but it never saw the light of day, because of the faults of the UAM. To give another type of example, the controversy over procedure which preceded the attempts to arbitrate the 1963 Nigerian-Dahomean conflict could have been settled in advance. After the 1962 conflict between Gabon and Congo-Brazzaville, the UAM Secretariat had proposed a legal formula for the settlement of disputes between states, a formula which envisioned a permanent Commission of Conciliation and a Court of Arbitration. The latter was to function according to precise rules of procedure and was to give legal form to decisions handed down in the presence of a conference of the heads of state. This project—whose object was also to avoid those annoyances which are forever being caused by arbitrations assigned in good faith to this or that individual—remained, alas, in the files of African chancelleries, which preferred to go on resorting to a process of improvisation whose inefficiency was amply demonstrated. Still another example of a failure of the UAM was on the question of bringing aid to those African countries not yet independent. In a document submitted to the heads of state at the Ouagadougou Conference, the Secretariat stated:

> What is interesting to note is that the UAM has limited itself to the diplomatic level alone in its "firm resolution" to come to the aid of the not yet independent African countries. At the UN, the most prominent and well-known representatives unanimously condemned the obsolete colonial policies of Spain and Portugal, as well as the racial policy in South Africa. This means simply that the "aid" is still kept on the level of public declarations; it is essentially an ideological aid. In the area of finance, as in the military and social sphere, this aid remains rather ineffectual; nevertheless, nationalists of Angola, Spanish Guinea, and the Rhodesias, to mention only a few, continue to ply the African continent. They make it known everywhere that they don't need proclamations as much as they need money. . . .

Despite this urgent appeal, the resolution adopted in regard to this problem at Ouagadougou stipulated without qualification but also without explanation of how the measure would be carried out: "The UAM heads of state hereby decide to take concrete measures to liquidate the remaining colonial forts in Africa." In reality nothing was done until Addis Ababa, when the UAM left to Algeria, Ghana, and Guinea the role of defender of the interests of African countries still under foreign domination.

Obstacles

Could the UAM, an organization of good will but having a rather loose structure, escape the accusation of being itself at the mercy of neo-colonialism? The greatest shortcoming of the UAM in diplomacy was the impression it sometimes gave of an excessive dependence on France. The ties between each of the UAM states and France were in effect so close as to give the impression that the organization itself drew its every inspiration from the former metropole. Certain member states put a great deal of effort into making their diplomatic positions agree with those of the French government. Most of the UAM heads of state tend to think of General de Gaulle as their "counselor" or "mentor." An amazing number of telegrams sometimes streamed from certain heads of state to the French government whenever De Gaulle obtained the least success. Furthermore, African heads of state passing Paris never failed to pay a visit to the General. This was an easily understandable act of courtesy, but the impression was that these visits were too frequent and that they sometimes took place before or after African conferences on international matters. Leaders in the countries of the British Commonwealth, such as Azikiwe, Tafawa Balewa, or Nkrumah, rarely make visits to London.

There was some truth in accusations about dependence on France. It was noticed that when De Gaulle spoke of "the Europe of Fatherlands," the UAM heads of state began talking about "the Africa of Fatherlands." At the Bangui Conference and after, the problem of relations with France was treated as a question of utmost importance for the organization.

Several states—taking into consideration their economic and financial position—wished to harmonize the policy of the UAM states with respect to France. But, to certain others, this plan of imitating the British Commonwealth was being initiated too late. These opponents of the plan saw it as a way of reviving the already defunct *Communauté* and opposed it violently. In the words of one of the leaders:

> Dear Colleagues, don't deceive yourselves. General de Gaulle does not harmonize his policy with anyone, neither with the Germans, nor with the Americans. What he is after is French prestige, which is quite understandable, but I seriously doubt that this prestige bears any relation to the well-defined interests of each of our states. It is for these reasons that I oppose personally a plan which would put us back in Paris, gathered about General de Gaulle, in order to receive a kind of sanction which we do not need and which African and international opinion would judge very unfavorably, *under present circumstances.*

Thus the plan for the development of relations between the UAM states and the French Republic was defeated.

On another occasion, the UAM heads of state did not seem to be blinded by their ties with France when, in good faith no doubt, it was proposed that French technical advisors be assigned to the African states for consultation during UN sessions. A UAM Commission was directed to study this question. Reporting for the Commission, Emile Zinsou summed up as follows:

> With regard to the question of technical assistance from the French government to the UAM, within the framework of the UN, the delegates consider on the whole that the use of French personnel is not desirable. For, psychologically, it would have a very bad effect on the reputation of the independence of the group. On the other hand, if France offered to furnish our common Secretariat with a documentation of the history of the UN and certain other questions on the daily agenda, it is certain that the group would accept this offer quite willingly. But, for the moment, it seems that technical aid from France cannot go beyond this point.

This conclusion was accepted unanimously by the heads of state.

It is hard to say what benefits could result from alternately showing more and then less independence. The reputation of being a group too closely bound to France certainly harmed the UAM's position in the United Nations. It was because of this that the states of this organization regularly found themselves excluded from the various commissions and from certain posts in the UN Secretariat. On this point a Gabonese report said: "It is distressing to have to state that, at the UN Disarmament Commission, to mention this example only, the five English-speaking countries of Africa south of the Sahara obtained two seats, while the twelve states of the UAM were simply and solely excluded."

In spite of obvious successes, which did not fail to alarm the Casablanca Group (whose verbal vigor outweighed concrete action), the UAM failed—through its own fault—to attain its goal of unity. In July, 1963, President Yameogo of Upper Volta, speaking in his capacity as acting President of the UAM, told the Cotonou Conference:

> So long as the UAM, which was present at Addis Ababa with the full weight of an influence recognized by the whole world, continues to take a path parallel to that of the OAU, all those startled by our unity, all the impenitent colonialists, who still think they can control from afar responsible heads of state as we are—all these, I repeat, might deliver a mortal blow to our unity. Consider the disgrace which will fall on our countries and friends, consider the heavy burden of responsibility we will have to bear in the face of history and future generations if one day the UAM has to be blamed for having torpedoed African Unity.

When even the acting President of the UAM implied that he feared those "who still think they can control from afar responsible heads of state as we are," then it is not surprising that President Sékou Touré denounced the organization as an "instrument in the hands of the partitioners of Africa," or, to be more precise, as an instrument of neo-colonialism tending to maintain the old privileges of the former colonial powers.

In short, the real problem of the UAM was that the success which it had—before dissolution at Dakar in March, 1964—came from its determination to do something about the harmful effects of balkanization. But that very balkanization created "client-states" or "vassal-states" having ties with the former colonial power. If the vassals regroup themselves only in order to coordinate several of their activities, without attacking the root of the problem by questioning their balkanized and feudalized "sovereignty," then it is clear that this process is not an expression of independence but is merely a new way of getting together to beg from the same overlord more effectively.

Africans sometimes like to point out that the existence of the Organization of American States does not at all hinder the continuation of the Monroe Doctrine, as a subtle way for the United States to exercise a kind of protectorate over the countries which occupy the rest of the Americas—in particular, several countries of Latin America. Counter-balkanization efforts in Africa, if they are to be only a slight corrective of dependency, cannot lead to the goal of true sovereignty.

[21]

On the contrary, if Africans limit themselves to patchwork compromises, they make of African unity nothing but an association of clients or a cooperative of consumers. Finally, of course, this severe analysis of the tragic failings of the UAM must take into consideration the fact that the organization was young and therefore forced to feel its way. And, it must also be remembered that, despite all these problems, major crises were sometimes faced with the highest degree of courage, and important achievements, particularly in communications, were accomplished.

III

The Administrative Secretariat

The legal basis of the Secretariat was laid down in Articles 2 and 3 of the UAM Charter. Article 2 states: "The UAM is founded on the solidarity uniting its members. Its goal is to organize the cooperation of its members in all domains of foreign policy, in order to reinforce their solidarity, to assure their collective security, to foster their economic development, to maintain peace in Africa, in Madagascar, and in the world." Article 3 states: "The UAM shall have a General Administrative Secretariat, with headquarters at Cotonou. The Administrative Secretary-General shall be named for two years by the Conference of Heads of State and Government, upon proposal of the President of the Republic of Dahomey. His salary shall be established by the same Conference, which also shall approve the annual budget of the General Administrative Secretariat. Each State's contribution to that budget shall be proportional to the operating budget of each member state."

These two articles give some idea of the scope of the tasks entrusted to the Secretary-General and the level of his responsibilities. The terms of the Charter, cast in this abstract form, however, tended to create delicate problems of daily application.

The position of the UAM in Africa and in the world has been sketched in the opening chapters. Its principal pacts and meetings have been mentioned, and something has been said about its characteristic operations. In succeeding chapters, the UAM's response to two crises is discussed in detail. Here, however, I would especially like to speak in the first person. To show how the organization's Secretary-General perceived his office may have some documentary value. In any case, issues which must be considered in a proper analysis of the Secretariat are those which engaged me deeply.

Christian Vierra of Dahomey had been the first Secretary-General, but he resigned after one month because of difficulties with the government of Dahomey. Therefore my first task was the practical organization of the Secretariat: the physical setup and, above all, the recruitment of personnel. First, I had to draw up a list of positions that seemed indispensable, spell out the qualifications required, provide for an adequate geographic distribution, and avoid recruiting personnel exterior to the organization (French technical advisors and others). The problem was not an easy one to solve, given the lack of cadres, chronic in African states.

After several weeks of discussions and reflections, I came up with the following organizational framework: Secretary-General; Deputy Secretary-General; Director of Administration and Finance; Legal Advisor; Director of the Department of Information and Cultural Affairs; Director of Technical Assistance Services, in charge of liaison in his field between states of the UAM and other African countries. To these top-level administrators were added: an executive assistant who accompanied me on all my trips; a special official in charge of Arab affairs; a press attaché; an accountant; seven secretaries; six maintenance personnel. The Secretariats of the UAM pact services each had more or less the same number of personnel.

Once the organizational framework had been set forth, it was necessary to fill the positions provided for. Considering the group of states making up the UAM, I decided to offer the post of Deputy Secretary-General to someone from the East, since I myself came from the West. Consequently, Germain Mba of Gabon was named Deputy Secretary-General of the UAM. His role was to take my place when I was absent, to take charge of relations with specialized organizations of the Union, international organizations, non-member African states, and non-African states desiring to establish relations on various levels with the UAM.

Of the other high-level positions, I wanted to offer one to Senegal, one to the Ivory Coast, one to Cameroon, and one to Malagasy. But because of the shortage of civil servants, this plan proved impossible. I obtained with difficulty a Senegalese—Amadou Dieng—who became Director of Administrative and Financial Affairs. His role was to prepare and oversee the execution of the budget, to look after personnel contracts, to prepare the various conferences on the administrative level. For several months, I persisted in requesting the governments in Abidjan and Tananarive to send the men I needed. Finally, I received a national of the Ivory Coast for Press Attaché. He remained only a few months in the Secretariat. He was replaced by a Madagascan, Hughes Rabesahala, who was to meet his death in a plane crash. Congo-Brazzaville loaned me temporarily Judge Louis Amegah, who served as Legal Advisor for eight weeks.

Under these circumstances, since work was piling up, I was compelled to rely upon Dahomeans. I named Albert Ekue Director of the Department of Information and Cultural Affairs. He had already worked with me when I was Minister of Information in Dahomey. His role consisted in publishing a weekly bulletin in collaboration with the Press Attaché, *La Semaine Africaine et Malgache*, and a quarterly review entitled *Nations Nouvelles*, in three editions — French, English, and Arabic. Finally, he was to keep the Secretariat informed on international news. A special post was reserved for attending to relations with the Arab world, and Didi Ould Sidi Ali, a Mauritanian official, was placed in charge.

I finally entrusted the posts of Legal Advisor and temporary Director of Technical Assistance Services to Maurice Glé-Lé, a Dahomean who had formerly served at UNESCO. His job was to draft the new documents we needed (e.g., on the settlement of disputes between states), to supervise the application of the agreements in force, and to draw up a system for cooperation on personnel, etc.

When it became absolutely essential to help our representatives at the UN by establishing a permanent Secretariat in New York, the government of Cameroon reluctantly agreed to send François Sengat-Kua to discharge this difficult responsibility. In general, all these officials were exemplary in their loyalty to the organization, and I did not note any signs of extreme nationalism. They were adequately paid and were zealous to the point of working Saturdays and Sundays when the need arose.

Indeed, the work facing us was both varied and absorbing. An ordinary day began at 8 A.M. and ended at 6 P.M., with two hours for lunch. Preparing and following up conferences took a great deal of our time. It must not be forgotten that the heads of state met twice annually and that meetings of experts and ministers were often called on problems of a precise technical nature (foreign affairs, budget, public service, etc.). Documents had to be prepared to serve as a basis for discussions; then commentaries, critiques, and resolutions had to be gathered, and dossiers were prepared for every state. Confidential documents, discussed in closed meetings attended exclusively by the heads of state, were the subject of special unpublished reports, for which I had sole responsibility.

Preparing for conferences often necessitated trips to find out what such and such a chief of state or important person thought about a problem relating to his country, his program, his preoccupations. All of this was part of the daily work. There were also what might be termed extraordinary activities: the settlement of the dispute between Gabon and Congo-Brazzaville, the accession of Rwanda to membership in the UAM, the Togolese question before and after the assassination of President Olympio, the setting up of the permanent Secretariat of the UAM in New York, etc.

Rwanda would never have joined the UAM had the Secretariat not taken a number of initiatives and risks. I believed that a loyalty to the UAM should not prevent me from acknowledging some of the positive criticisms leveled against the organization. I was personally disturbed by the fact that the UAM seemed to numerous observers—

not all of whom were bitter or malicious—to be a club of former French colonies which had remained faithful to their metropole rather than an African organization open to the continent. At that time, there was a good deal of thought given to the possibility of holding a meeting in Paris between the heads of state of the UAM and General de Gaulle, for the purpose of harmonizing Franco-African relations beyond the fictitious existence of the *Communauté*, to which several states still theoretically belonged.

I was not alone in thinking that in view of the divergences with the Casablanca Group and the irritation that certain English-speaking partners of the Monrovia Group were increasingly expressing, this scheduled meeting in Paris would have been a psychological error and a political mistake. The British Commonwealth did indeed have historical and universal scope, "with only silken ties," as Nehru said, but analogies between it and the relationship of France with the UAM could not stand up under serious examination. Therefore, I accepted eagerly a mission entrusted to me by President Ahmadou Ahidjo of Cameroon, also at that time President of the UAM. I was to enter into contact with the government of Rwanda and to study on the spot the possibilities of cooperation with this former Belgian colony.

If Rwanda, which had never been a French colony, would adhere to the UAM, to my mind it was a great step toward an Africanization of the organization, a means of establishing a certain psychological distance vis-à-vis Paris, an argument for not meeting with French officials before the 1963 conference in Addis Ababa. Had such a meeting taken place, it would definitely have given weight to the accusations made by the organization's enemies.

I obtained the confidence of the heads of state without difficulty on this particular problem, and I succeeded in persuading President Grégoire Kayibanda of Rwanda not only to come to the conference of the UAM in Libreville but also to join the organization before the conference of Addis Ababa. The time devoted to this question was long, the missions numerous, and the collection of information taxing.

In the same period, a rapprochement took place between the UAM and Congo-Leopoldville, under the government of Cyrille Adoula. It was the time of the Katanga secession. The support this secession received from President Youlou is well known—while the other heads of state demonstrated a marked preference for the central government.

The working rules of the UAM required that the position of Congo-Brazzaville be taken into account. Since general consent is required for all important questions, the right of veto was in effect accorded to President Youlou in all matters relating to the Congo. However, after the assassination of Patrice Lumumba, the mysterious death of Dag Hammarskjöld, and the multiple *volte-faces* of Moise Tshombe, the position of the Katanga leader became increasingly diffi-

[26]

cult, and Youlou grew less and less convinced that his ally would win. No member-state of the UAM—even Malagasy, which was closer to Tshombe's ideas than to those of Leopoldville—recognized the Katanga regime. France, while displaying an obliging attitude (some of the mercenaries recruited by Tshombe were French), maintained a prudent distance officially.

U Thant's plan for the reunification of the Congo, which was accepted by both Leopoldville and Elisabethville, won wide acceptance in international opinion. At that point, in July, 1962, the Secretariat of the UAM undertook a new initiative in regard to the Congo. The Leopoldville government was a member of the Monrovia Group. I hoped that a rapprochement might be possible between the central government and the UAM, now that Youlou's ally Tshombe was increasingly losing his control over Katanga and now that he had agreed at least officially to the plan for reunification proposed by the United Nations. After conferring with President Ahidjo in his capacity at that time as head of the UAM, I made a personal trip to see President Youlou, to explain to him the important role he could play in Central Africa. If the Congo-Leopoldville were associated with the UAM, it would provide a prime opportunity for the leader from Brazzaville— so close—to play arbiter, conciliator, and to strengthen his position in Africa. Youlou agreed immediately to the project; he also looked favorably on our overtures to Rwanda.

On the strength of President Youlou's support and with authorization from President Ahidjo, I went to Leopoldville, where Adoula and Bomboko agreed, after 24 hours of detailed discussion, to the principle of an immediate association with the UAM and gave me a long letter confirming this agreement. The Leopoldville government thus seized the opportunity offered to it to enlarge its circle of friends, to seek economic and eventually military cooperation—in order to give the Congo a new image.

Justin Bomboko represented the Leopoldville government at the Libreville Conference, where the UAM-Congo agreements were to be sealed, and he aroused great enthusiasm when he declared:

> If certain political options have at times separated us, it nonetheless remains true that our place is very naturally at your side. Of course, certain of our closest friends have occasionally hesitated over the path to follow and misunderstood our acts and our intentions.[1] This sorry epoch is henceforth of the past, and if I mention it, it is to say that it will in no wise impede our will to succeed nor our firm will to collaborate with you.

Following the Libreville Conference, a convention was drawn up

---

[1]An evident allusion to Youlou, who, despite his promises, had included a Katanga Senator in his delegation to the Libreville Conference. The latter was dismissed without very great trouble.

to provide the former Belgian colony with the middle-level cadres it needed, and financial resources were sought. But, unfortunately, the project bore no concrete results, mainly because: (1) the Congolese administration never furnished the statement of its needs that was requested; (2) the UAM was, at that time, itself in the throes of an administrative crisis and thus could not assure a continuity in its operations; and (3) the new tensions in the Congo Republic hardly inspired enthusiasm among the middle-level cadres who were to serve there.

The growing importance of the Secretariat caused difficulties in my relations with certain chiefs of state, particularly with Hubert Maga. Maga was inclined to be highly distrustful of his friends or collaborators, if he thought they were too well known or were capable of constituting a force that would diminish his own. Maga became President of Dahomey completely by accident. Hence, he was never certain of what the next day would bring, and he feared like the plague anyone inside or outside Dahomey capable of overshadowing him. We had nonetheless been close friends: after the proclamation of independence, I had offered him my collaboration and that of several intellectuals from the South. (At that time, partly because Maga was from the North, he encountered a forceful opponent in the person of Justin Ahomadegbe.) Further, Maga had never taken Vice-President Sourou-Migan Apithy into confidence but, instead, had preferred to push him aside by naming him Ambassador to France. This aspect of Maga's personality manifested itself violently in the crises I had to deal with during the years 1962–63. Because the Charter of the UAM specified in Article 3 that the Secretary-General should be named upon proposal of the President of the Republic of Dahomey, Maga thought he could make a personal affair out of this post. I was to inform him of details, advise him before I departed on missions, submit press communiqués to him, etc.

The issue of a communiqué on the Round Table Conference called to settle Gabon's dispute with Congo-Brazzaville was the beginning of open conflict between Maga and me. Maga was not present in the capital but nonetheless complained that he had not been notified by telephone before the publication of this communiqué, and he expressed his astonishment that the Dahomean suggestion to call an extraordinary conference of the heads of state of the UAM had been dismissed. He refused to go to Douala and circulated most tendentious comments. Nonetheless, several of the other heads of state supported me vigorously, notably Senghor, Ahidjo, and Leon Mba. The participants at Douala even sent an official letter to Maga, inviting him thereafter to offer me his cooperation.

Despite this active support, Maga posed the problem of the Secretary-General during the Ouagadougou Conference. He was seconded by his colleagues from the Conseil de l'Entente. The discussion

[28]

took place behind closed doors, in my absence, and I was not allowed to defend myself. The most fantastic and ridiculous accusations were raised. One of the heads of state advised me to resign, after confiding that Maga had threatened to withdraw from the organization if I remained at the head of the Secretariat. I had no choice. I left the Secretariat of the UAM.

Bertrand Dagnon of Dahomey succeeded me. Barely five weeks later, he was killed in a plane crash. Max Zollner, also of Dahomey, was then appointed Secretary-General, and he remained in the post for eight months, until the transformation of the UAM into the UAMCE (discussed in Chap. VI).

As for Maga, six months after my resignation, he was no longer President. He was removed from power suddenly by a joint revolt of the people, the unions, and the army.

IV

The Dispute Between Gabon
and Congo-Brazzaville

Among the many problems which the UAM faced, the 1962 dispute between Congo-Brazzaville and Gabon deserves particular attention. It was one of those innumerable results of balkanization with which Africa seems destined to become ever more familiar.

BACKGROUND

Next to Congo-Brazzaville lies Gabon, a country half the size of France but with scarcely 500,000 inhabitants. Gabon is enormously wealthy in natural resources, including *okoumé* (a valuable wood used in the plywood industry), diamonds, iron ore, manganese, uranium, gold, and oil. Gabon is one of the few African countries where the value of exports exceeds that of imports. In 1961 exports amounted to about 14 billion francs CFA, whereas imports totaled about 9 billion.

It was at Libreville in Gabon that the Commissariat for the French Congo had its headquarters until 1910. Up to 1920, the colony of Gabon, which was the point of French penetration of Central Africa, included Upper Ogoué. In 1925 the French decided for reasons of administrative convenience, associated with the building of the Congo-Ocean railway, to attach Upper Ogoué to the colony of Central Congo, in the same way that in West Africa Upper Volta was later attached for a time to the Ivory Coast.

In 1946, at the insistence of the Gabonese and with the agreement of the deputy for the Congo, Felix Tchikaya, Upper Ogoué was reunited administratively to Gabon by a decree of the French government. A few years afterward the prodigious economic development of Franceville gave the Congolese cause to regret their having let it go. On the other hand, the Gabonese never forgave the former Federation of French Equatorial Africa for developing Brazzaville and Pointe-Noire at Gabon's expense. In October, 1962, President Mba remarked that:

Gabon is without a road worthy of the name, without a railroad, even

[30]

though the French parliament voted credits for a railway from Owendo to Ouesso in 1906. Gabon has no port, despite the important contribution of its resources to the general infrastructures [of the AEF] created outside our country.

The bitterness of the Gabonese leaders at the time of the 1956 *loi-cadre* frustrated all attempts at unification, federation, or even confederation. Like Abidjan, Libreville did not wish to be a milch cow and preferred to opt for a "balkanization" ostensibly favorable to Gabon. Certain crucial problems, however, remained unsolved. With scarcely 500,000 inhabitants, Gabon lacked an adequate work-force for industry, which found itself forced to look elsewhere for manual laborers. Thousands of Congolese, unable to find work in their own country, poured into Gabon, where they were often highly thought of by their European and Gabonese employers. This situation did not delight the native population. Nothing was done to improve living conditions for the "foreign" workers, who complained that they worked night and day and lived in hovels.

In September, 1962, a year after its creation at Tananarive, the UAM met at Libreville, under the increasing attention of an international audience. President Kayibanda came to Libreville in person and began negotiations for Rwanda membership in the UAM. Congo-Leopoldville sent Justin Bomboko, at that time Foreign Minister. Burundi, with extreme timidity, sent an official of the Ministry of Health. Representatives of various nationalist organizations in Angola, Rhodesia, Spanish Guinea, and Portuguese Guinea also sent delegates to Libreville, and President Sékou Touré not only sent a message to the conference but also sent his ambassador in residence at Lagos to convey both his support and interest. Messages expressing greeting and congratulations were received from Pope John XXIII, General de Gaulle, President Kennedy, the King of Morocco, and several other important personages.

The Libreville Conference was a great success, and President Mba, who had arranged it, was elected President of the UAM. The conference ended on September 13, and Mba had barely taken up his responsibilities when five days later the most serious political conflict the UAM was to know burst like a storm out of a clear, blue sky.

THE FOOTBALL RIOTS

During the Cup of the Tropics Competition, the Gabonese soccer teams claimed they had been ill-treated. Certain Europeans who had been watching stated, when questioned, that the attitude of the Congolese toward the Gabonese was not unusual, that there had been, as there often were, a few insults and skirmishes and some stone-throwing, but nothing very serious. Indeed, after the games, a brilliant reception had been given at the "Cascade" in Brazzaville under the kind patronage of M. N'Zalakanda, then Minister of the Interior, with the intention of erasing bad feelings. However, the Gabonese public and the Gabonese government were given an absolutely horrifying account of what had taken place in Brazzaville, and this touched off the explosion.

At about the same time, the President of the Congo Republic had sent his Minister of Labor, Faustin Okomba, to gather information about the conditions of Congolese workers in Gabon. Congo-Brazzaville maintained that it had given official notice to the Gabonese authorities of Minister Okomba's mission, while Gabon categorically denied this. During a press conference at Libreville on October 3, 1962, President Mba stated:

> Without having obtained the agreement of the Gabonese government, the government of Congo-Brazzaville decided unilaterally to send its Minister of Labor on an official mission to Gabon to make inquiries among the Congolese who had come to our country recently to find work. The Gabonese government, which does not regard itself as an administrative province of the Congo, has been unable to regard this action as anything but unfriendly and outrageous. . . .

A letter, which was presented as evidence during an inquiry conducted by the General Secretariat of the UAM in Brazzaville, showed clearly that the matter in question was indeed a unilateral act on the part of the Congolese authorities. President Youlou had written: "I have decided to send Minister Okomba on a mission to Gabon. . . ." Gabon had simply been informed of the Congo Republic's intention, and President Youlou had not requested authorization for his Minister of Labor either to travel in a foreign country or to make inquiries there.

In short, the arrival of Minister Okomba annoyed the Gabonese government, which was all the more disposed to believe the stories told by the soccer players on their return from Brazzaville. A great deal was made of leaflets which had been distributed before the game in the Congolese capital. Here is a sample of their inflammatory prose:

> The great day has come!
> The terrible Gabonese are at our gates!
> They have come to butcher our sons and our women!

Hotheads in Libreville interpreted the experience of the Gabonese footballers as a Congolese provocation deserving vengeance. Dormant emotional issues between the peoples of the two countries suddenly sprang into life, and on the night of September 19 four Congolese and five Gabonese died, and many were injured. A whole section inhabited by Congolese was set afire and completely burned down. Not one stone was left standing in another. Minister Okomba was saved just in the nick of time and escorted to an aircraft by the police.

On September 20, drastic measures, including a curfew from 7 P.M. to 6 A.M., were taken to maintain public order in Libreville. Fearing that the anti-Congolese movement might reach the interior of the country, Gabon decided to repatriate Congolese workers and requested as a reciprocal measure that the Congolese government should "repatriate" all Gabonese resident in the Congo.[1] Meanwhile sporting events between the two countries had been suspended, and President Youlou had made an official appeal to General de Gaulle to settle the dispute.

The day the repatriated Congolese disembarked was declared a day of mourning in Brazzaville, and several religious services were held. Among the first repatriates to arrive at Pointe-Noire some were injured, others were barely clothed. At this point, a wave of fury swept through the population of Pointe-Noire, where no particular security precautions had been taken. All "foreigners" were fair game as a wave of xenophobia swept through the Congo. Many Gabonese, Dahomeans, Togolese, Nigerians, and Cameroonians fell victim to the popular fury, and the repatriation of foreigners to their own countries became inevitable.

The heads of state of the UAM appealed in vain for calm and common sense. As Secretary-General of the UAM, I was sent on an information-gathering mission to Libreville, where I was received by President Mba and had a frank and relaxed discussion. Though still angry and regretful about the brutalities, the Gabonese President stated that he was ready for a reconciliation and proposed that an effort be made to settle the dispute. I then left immediately for Pointe-Noire which had been the scene of the most serious incidents in the Congo. At the airport there were men, women, and children camped everywhere, awaiting evacuation. In Brazzaville, in the absence of President Youlou, the UAM delegation was received by Minister Okomba and Minister N'Zalakanda. They gave their approval to the initiative of the UAM in settling the dispute, but Youlou's attitude was still unknown.

As has already been pointed out, the other "foreigners" living in the Congo—Dahomeans, Nigerians, Togolese—had suffered as much if not more than the Gabonese, against whom the action had first been intended. In Dahomey the National Assembly met and adopted a "vigorous" resolution, as follows:

> Considering the expression of deep grief and the alarming condition of the 142 Dahomean repatriates who arrived on Sunday, October 30, 1962, and the 600 awaited at any moment,
> Considering that the Dahomeans were not the cause of these regrettable incidents in Gabon,

---

[1]This measure was severely criticized in all the UAM states because it constituted a violation of the Convention d'Établissement signed by all members.

Considering the membership of the Republic of Dahomey in the UAM, which was created for the realization of African unity,

This Assembly:

1. Pays tribute to the French forces stationed at Pointe-Noire.
2. Registers a strong protest and expresses its profound indignation at the provocations and inexcusable aggressions perpetrated by the Congolese on Dahomean citizens.

With the encouragement of public opinion in his country President Maga called for an extraordinary session of the heads of state of the UAM. After discussion with me, however, he agreed to a more restrained solution, providing for a Round Table Conference at which the principal interested parties would be present.

Getting President Youlou to consent was more difficult. He refused to agree to a Round Table Conference in Abidjan, since he did not see why "a ruler of the former AOF should lay down the law for heads of state of the former AEF [sic], even if this ruler were M. Houphouet-Boigny, President of the Rassemblement Démocratique Africain."² However he gave his agreement to a conference in Cameroon on the condition that François Tombalbaye, President of Chad and at the time also President of the UDE, would take the initiative.³ A Round Table Conference was finally arranged for November 3 at Douala, Cameroon, with Youlou, Mba, Tombalbaye, Ahidjo, Maga, President Hamani Diori of Niger, and a representative of Houphouet-Boigny.

A few days later, at Cotonou, in replying to a journalist's question about why all the heads of state of the UAM were not meeting, as Dahomey wished, I pointed out that the Charter of the UAM provided that the request for an extraordinary session had to be supported by a majority of the members of the organization. Since this had not yet been obtained, it had been necessary to find another formula

---

²It will be recalled that former French West Africa (AOF) was comprised of: Mauritania, Senegal, Upper Volta, Mali, Niger, Guinea, the Ivory Coast, and Dahomey. French Equatorial Africa (AEF) was comprised of: Central Congo (Congo-Brazzaville), Ubangi-Chari (Central African Republic), Chad, and Gabon. The former AOF had benefited more from opportunities for promotion than the former AEF. This difference in opportunity was often translated into rivalry on different levels.

The Rassemblement Démocratique Africain (RDA) was a political party with members in various African countries. President Youlou was a member, as was President Mba.

³As a consequence of the autonomy accorded to the African territories by the *loi-cadre* of Gaston Defferre, the federations of the AOF and AEF had gradually disappeared. To maintain the economic ties existing between the former territories of French Equatorial Africa, the UDE, had been created, a kind of economic community, the presidency of which was assigned in turn to the heads of state of the various members.

quickly. Unfortunately, this purely bureaucratic reply provoked another minor crisis. Presidents Maga and David Dacko of the Central African Republic, both of whom had advocated different formulas, refused to go to Douala.

THE ROUND TABLE CONFERENCE AT DOUALA

When President Ahidjo opened the Round Table Conference on November 3, 1962, he requested the two heads of the disputing countries to express frankly "everything they had in their hearts," in the higher interests of the UAM.

President Youlou spoke first:

> I must confess to you that I have nothing particular to say. I plead guilty in advance. . . . President Leon Mba has prepared documents and dossiers, and I prefer him to set forth his point of view and that members of the Commission question me afterwards. I shall answer as best I can. . . .

President Mba, paying no heed to the tactical maneuver by his opponent, spent two hours on a detailed account of relations between Congo-Brazzaville and Gabon over several years. Mba presented facts to support his charge that certain members of the Congolese government were seeking by every means at their disposal to annex the Franceville area of Gabon. Mba claimed that since 1959 Gabonese residents in the Congo who returned to Gabon were in possession of authorizations issued by the Congolese government for the purchase of arms and that it had been *unofficially* intimated to them that this mark of favor was meant to show them and their families still in Gabon the high regard and political interest the Congo felt for them. In certain cases, he asserted, deputies of the Congo Republic had acted as intermediaries for the transfer of these arms.

President Mba disclosed further that in July, 1960, a Nigerian named Aladji Amadou Raji, later identified as an envoy of the cabinet of the President of Congo-Brazzaville, made a journey into the interior of Gabon in a car which had been placed at his disposal by the Congolese government. Intercepted in the north, at Oyem, and found in possession of a revolver, this individual was sent back to Dolisie. In response to a letter identified as No. 1139 of August 26, 1960, from the President of the Congo Republic, Gabon returned the car to the Congolese government as a gesture of friendship.

Further, according to President Mba, in April, 1960, Anselme Kouka, who was in charge of propaganda within President Youlou's party, had supposedly invited a certain number of Gabonese nationals living in Brazzaville to his home and asked them to recruit and pay literate natives of Upper Ogoué to engage in propaganda favoring the area's annexation by the Congo. At the conclusion of the meeting, M.

[35]

Kouka had supposedly taken the Gabonese to the Brazzaville city hall for a reception by President Youlou, who informed them that Upper Ogoué had been "sold" to Gabon by the former deputy Tchikaya and that this area now had to return to the Congo.

President Mba made a further statement concerning what he called "irrefutable facts." A Gabonese named Armand Ombana had stated that the President of the Congo Republic had remitted considerable sums (2,500,000 francs CFA) to a Gabonese politician, a native of Upper Ogoué, to gain his support for Congolese territorial claims. Confronted with M. Ombana, this Gabonese politician, while disputing the large sums, did acknowledge having received funds from President Youlou during private conversations which had taken place in the Presidential palace in Brazzaville on the occasion of the Congolese national holiday in November, 1961.[4]

Giving more details of his accusations, Gabon's President stated that M. Goyi, head of the Congolese Minister of Finance's staff, had established dubious political contacts while on a journey to Libreville in May, 1961. Moreover, M. Goura, Minister of Finance of Congo-Brazzaville and Mayor of Dolisie, had stayed in the Ngounie area for two weeks in June, 1960, during the elections to rural organizations, without having informed the Gabonese government or the Prefectorial authorities in advance.

According to the Libreville authorities, this collection of reports, all in agreement with each other, proved that the President of the Congo Republic had tried to stimulate agitation in Upper Ogoué and had used methods which could not be justified between two friendly countries sharing the same ideal of African brotherhood and solidarity. Furthermore, added President Mba, in the course of the UAM conference in Libreville, Youlou and Stephane Tchichelle had taken advantage of Gabonese hospitality to multiply their "dubious" contacts among Congolese residents in Libreville, "encouraging demands and working to arouse agitation."

President Mba finished his speech by reading a letter of September 29, 1962, sent to him by the French Ambassador in Libreville, on the situation of the Gabonese in the Congo:

At *Pointe-Noire:* gathered at the airfield, 1,600 Dahomeans, 500 Gabonese, 200 Cameroonians, 100 Togolese, 100 unspecified.

At *Brazzaville:* also gathered at the airfield, 417 Gabonese, 81 Cameroonians, 48 Dahomeans, 34 Togolese, 12 Ghanaians.

At *Dolisie:* about 500 Gabonese protected by the police.

At *Jacob:* 20 to 25 Gabonese under the protection of the police.

---

[4]All the indications are that the Gabonese in question here is M. Amogho, today Minister of Public Works in the Mba government.

As you know, the Congolese authorities remain opposed to compulsory mass repatriation of Gabonese. They are giving authorizations to those who ask to leave for Gabon.

After the Gabonese leader had concluded his account with an appeal for conciliation and reasonableness, President Youlou rose solemnly and asked that silent homage be rendered to the dead. He then answered a few questions, but it was already late, and the session had to be brought to an end. The next day the Congolese President, who had stated the day before that he had no dossier prepared, distributed to the members of the conference over a hundred pages of documents, and the Gabonese then realized that the Congolese had led them to use up all their material so that they would be able to control the key position at the conference.

President Youlou relied essentially on a few points which were according to him "unassailable." He began as follows.

1. The Gabonese had been the first to unleash the conflict, with arson, murder, and serious injuries. Whatever the account presented by the soccer players to the Gabonese government, that government had no right whatever to take up a position without a more thorough investigation, and it should not have tolerated, furthermore, those disorders which had cost the lives of several Congolese.

2. By taking the initiative in repatriating all Congolese resident in Gabon, even for security reasons, the government in Libreville had deliberately broken the Convention d'Établissement signed at Tananarive between the states of the UAM. Youlou added that the fact that the President of Gabon was also the President of the UAM clearly showed "the risks of all supranational groupings or organizations, when one saw a ruling president shake the columns of the temple himself," at a time when he should be serving as a detached judge, entrusted with the task of supervising respect for the rules and the spirit of unity.

3. The Congolese government had serious reasons for sending a mission to Libreville to gather information on the situation of the Congolese workers, whose living conditions were not always bearable and who were bombarding their government with proposals and complaints. The Congolese government had sent a telegram to President Mba, informing him of the arrival of Minister Okomba, who was to hand to the head of the Gabonese government an explanatory message from the President of the Congo Republic. Mba had not deigned to receive Okomba.

4. Regarding the accusations concerning Franceville, President Youlou stated that one of the reasons for the UAM's existence was precisely to learn about disputes likely to break out between members of the organization. It was regrettable that the Union as such had not been informed in advance, and long in advance, of Gabon's

grievances, which had now been publicly exposed but which could have been made known well before the incidents, thus without doubt avoiding them. By preferring the method of the *fait accompli,* Gabon had precluded all means of arbitration, even those applicable in desperate cases.

5. Therefore, the Congolese government placed the material and moral responsibility for the damage suffered both in Gabon and in the Congo, "where the events had, alas, unfortunate repercussions," squarely on the shoulders of the Gabonese government.

This line of argument, firmly constructed, disturbed the members of the conference considerably. However, the conference forced the Congolese President to admit the difficulty of placing on the shoulders of Gabon the responsibility for all the damage done in the Congo, particularly when it was remembered that the authorities of Pointe-Noire had shown a gross dereliction of duty in organizing security measures. President Youlou continued to insist on his point of view, and his intransigence paid off, for Congo-Brazzaville did not accept the clause for the indemnification of the victims until after a formal promise had been given that all the states of the UAM would subscribe a certain share of the indemnity.

After all the explanations had been given, after the opposing parties had agreed in the higher interests of the African community to put an end to their conflict, the final communiqué of the Douala Conference read as follows:

Having concluded a general discussion, the Conference has expressed unanimously its heartfelt regret for the incidents which have brought such serious social consequences in their train both for Gabon and the Congo Republic.

The governments of the Congo Republic and Gabon deeply deplore the situation thus created and affirm that they are resolved to effect a final reconciliation and to normalize the good relations which they have always enjoyed in the past.

To this end, the two states of the Congo and Gabon accept the principle of indemnifying fairly all those who have suffered within their territories both in their persons and in their property.

The two governments solemnly declare that all the non-nationals of their states who have returned to their own countries may freely return to the Congo and to Gabon and resume their activities and their employment.

The Round Table Conference of Douala has noted with pleasure that the two governments of the Congo and Gabon have reaffirmed their complete adherence to all the principles and agreements of the UDE and of the UAM, particularly: the Founding Charter and the free circulation of persons and goods, respecting duly the sovereignty and territorial integrity of each state.

[38]

This last clause, "respecting duly the sovereignty and territorial integrity of each state," was inserted particularly to satisfy the Gabonese and to give warning to the Congo Republic regarding the Franceville area.

At a large public rally at the end of the conference, Presidents Mba and Youlou exchanged a fraternal embrace and extended mutual invitations for official visits to each other's country. The dispute between Congo-Brazzaville and Gabon had found a solution within the UAM. It was a typical case of those frontier squabbles born of balkanization. The settlement of this dispute was achieved without an appeal to General de Gaulle, as President Youlou had first requested. Dealing with this appeal for arbitration by General de Gaulle, President Mba had stated, not without humor, in his press conference of October 3: "We believe that the authority and moral grandeur of General de Gaulle in Africa and in the world at large are such that it would not be suitable to ask him to intervene in a dispute so petty and so limited."

THE LESSON OF THE CRISIS

The final communiqué of the Round Table Conference on the dispute between Congo-Brazzaville and Gabon calls, nevertheless, for a certain number of comments.

The pragmatic spirit reigning at the meeting at Douala had shown: (1) the absence of juridical standards within the UAM for the solution of crises of the kind just analyzed; (2) the uselessness of slogans about unity in the creation of communities integrated in depth, which might avoid tribalism and its tragic consequences. As a result, I focused on two plans: one providing for a permanent Commission for the conciliation of disputes and a Court of Arbitration; the other aiming at a closer association of the populace in each country with the efforts of their heads of state for African unity.

This project was welcomed when the heads of state next assembled in Ouagadougou, in March, 1963. They decided that Senegal, whose former Supreme Court President, M. Forster, is at present a judge on the International Court of Justice at The Hague, would produce a study of arbitration procedures after having collected all the comments and suggestions of the states who would be party to the proposed agreement. Unfortunately, administrative delays did not allow an agreement to be drawn up rapidly enough to eliminate the inefficiencies which were again encountered in the settlement of the 1963 dispute between Niger and Dahomey over various classes of workers who had been expelled from Niamey.

Plainly, law does not always suffice for the diagnosis and cure of social and political disturbances. This is why the Secretariat of the

UAM came to the conclusion that the populace must be more closely associated with the building up of African unity. We drew up a report asserting that African unity was believed to be a vital necessity by the heads of state, that the initiative had been taken at the top, but that the mass of the populace still remained behind.

As a step toward bringing all classes of the population to share more in the efforts of the heads of state to join together in building a united Africa, it was proposed that a committee of support for the UAM should be organized in each country. This committee would be a sounding board for the decisions of the heads of state. It would have the task of foreseeing and preventing conflicts and of safeguarding the interests of African unity. In each capital the committee would be comprised of representatives of youth movements, sections of the national party, sports associations, politicians, and eminent foreigners and natives. It would set up sub-sections in other important towns and villages. The participation of all social classes was not only desirable but necessary.

Further proposals were made for sporting events to stimulate understanding, mutual aid, and brotherhood and for cultural events likewise be organized with prizes (a prize for African Unity, for example) at various levels. Within the same framework it was decided to organize and nurture the pairing of cities among the various countries. It was also noted that women's discussion forums could be arranged, having as their aim the eventual formation of a Women's Organization for the UAM. Finally, a UAM Day was suggested as a symbol to bring about a UAM spirit in all social classes.

These were the organizational and psychological measures suggested after the dispute between Gabon and Congo-Brazzaville. The aim was to make good the deficiencies and close certain gaps in the institutional system of the UAM. Unfortunately, they were not put into practice. Nevertheless the fact that the UAM was able to absorb this crisis without external assistance was certainly a great success for the organization. In this case, it succeeded in preserving its solidarity and cohesiveness. It was not to do so in the face of the Togolese crisis.

V

The Togo Crisis

TERRITORIAL CONFLICT

Togo is a French-speaking African state having characteristics that led the UAM to watch it closely. To be sure, President Sylvanus Olympio of Togo looked askance at anything in Africa representing or recalling French colonization. But he was obliged to maintain ties not only with his French-speaking neighbors but with France as well (notably in currency matters). Furthermore, difficulties with Ghana made Togo more distrustful of the Casablanca Group and led it to opt in favor of the Monrovia Group, despite the close personal friendship between Olympio and Sékou Touré. Finally, it must be noted that Olympio's opponents had sought refuge in countries other than Ghana—they were also in Dahomey (Grunitzky), in Senegal (Ajavon), and in the Ivory Coast (Meatchi). All this must be taken into consideration in order to understand the UAM's interest in Togo, even though Olympio had never set foot in the Palais Bourbon and preferred to speak English at Pan-African conferences.

Although Togo had been a trust territory of the UN, France tried to maintain for as long as possible its trusteeship. While the French found in Nicolas Grunitzky the man of the moment for their policy, Olympio had support in the deep feelings of the Togolese people for independence and reunification of Togoland. But as to the latter subject, Olympio had to reckon with another leader of stature, Kwame Nkrumah, who was organizing the masses in the neighboring Gold Coast and who aimed to make the Gold Coast into a cell of Pan-Africa. When British Togo voted in a referendum under international control to be assimilated into Ghana, the Togolese did not conceal their disappointment, and the first difficulties appeared between Nkrumah and Olympio, who had earlier linked their struggle.

Having "lost" British Togo, Sylvanus Olympio succeeded on April 27, 1960, in proclaiming the independence of his own country, a tiny territory of 55,000 square kilometers (of which the capital is Lomé) with less than 2 million population and scanty revenues derived from copra and potassium. But if Olympio resigned himself then to managing his own Togo, Nkrumah did not lose sight of his Pan-African project and the promises which his Togolese colleagues may have made during the time of their common struggle. Border incidents grew in number. Statements became more and more heated. People traveling from one country to the other were subjected to long delays and numerous annoyances. In order to put pressure on Togo, Nkrumah entered into special relations with Dahomey, which Olympio had held at some distance.

In this general climate of tension and intrigues, I chanced to meet in Niamey in December, 1961, Nana Nketia, Vice-Chancellor of the University of Accra and cultural counselor to President Nkrumah, whom he was representing at the festivities marking the anniversary of the independence of the Republic of Niger. Nketia had also been a delegate, several days earlier, at Dar es Salaam at the festivities marking the independence of Tanganyika (attended also by Olympio). I was immediately drawn to this charming, serious, and determined man, and we spoke frankly of the problem of relations between Ghana and Togo. He also told me that Nkrumah wished for a rapprochement with the states of the UAM in order to advance his ideas on African unity. After discussion, we agreed to propose that President Maga of Dahomey arbitrate the Togo-Ghana conflict. Dahomey seemed well placed for the task, since it was neither the client nor the adversary of either party.

The next day I reported the discussion to President Maga, who was very open to the idea. I prepared a dossier on the affair and set out on a private visit to Accra. Nkrumah received me personally, and, after a probing discussion, we agreed that:

(1) Maga and Nkrumah would hold a preliminary meeting in northern Dahomey;

(2) Another meeting, again on Dahomean territory, would be arranged a short time later between Nkrumah, Olympio, and Maga;

(3) Ghana would sustain an interest in certain plans for economic development in Dahomey.

My contribution was finished. The official diplomatic consultations were to begin, and that was not in my province. I left for Dakar, in the line of my official duties. On my return to Cotonou ten days later, things had changed a great deal. The meeting between Maga and Nkrumah was no longer to be held in Dahomey, but at Pusiga, in northern Ghana.

I suspected then that my friend Dei Anang, Counselor to President Nkrumah for African Affairs, was at the root of this change in program, which I had opposed at all costs when I was in Accra. To my way of thinking, since President Maga had already made one

[42]

official visit to Ghana, it seemed irregular for him to take the road there a second time. But the die was cast. Considering the objectives, it was necessary to accept, all the more so in that President Maga had already agreed to the new plan.

It was evening when we arrived in Pusiga, where our visit was supposed to take place in complete seclusion. To our great surprise, when we crossed Togo, authorities had already been informed and had sent soldiers and policemen in order to facilitate "the passage through Togolese territory of the convoy of the President of Dahomey." In Pusiga itself, we were surprised to note that the population had been gathered to applaud and that photographers were everywhere. President Maga showed some annoyance but succeeded in containing himself.

Nkrumah received us cordially in a large classroom of the principal school, and we had a very positive work session. We spoke first of African unity as a fundamental idea. Nkrumah said that although he had always advocated that sovereign nationalities be merged to the benefit of one sole central government for Africa, he might be willing to modify his plan and accept the borders of the independent states for the moment, provided that we all undertake immediately a procedure for concerted diplomacy and coordinated defense. Maga found this plan interesting and little different from the objectives of the UAM. In conclusion, it was decided that the President of Dahomey should give a press conference upon his return to Cotonou on this conception of African unity and that Nkrumah would develop his new ideas on the subject before Ghana's Parliament. This undertaking seemed important for the Dahomean delegates, in that for the first time, publicly, Nkrumah would renounce any territorial ambitions on Togo in accepting the independence of the African countries within their present boundaries. Moreover, Nkrumah accepted willingly the idea of going to Dahomey to meet with Olympio and end the conflict. He told us, however, that he had no confidence in his colleague from Lomé and that he accepted reconciliation partly in order that the good efforts of the Dahomean statesmen should not be wasted.

For those of us from Dahomey, these harsh judgments on Olympio were less important than the prospect of reconciliation between Togo and Ghana. We had obtained promises to that effect; the rest lay in the realm of individual action. Finally, before ending the meeting, there was a discussion on Dahomey's plans for economic development and of a prospective participation of Ghana in these plans.

Several days after the meeting in Pusiga, Nkrumah kept his word on one essential point. He declared his further views on African unity before the Parliament in Accra, thus offering an accommodation with Togo on the eve of a conference of the Monrovia Group in Lagos.

In the meantime, I had been sent to Lomé, where I was to be

[43]

received on Sunday morning, January 21, 1962, by the President. Upon arrival, I learned that Olympio had just escaped an attempt on his life. This news intensified my conviction that it was necessary at all costs to succeed in reconciling Ghana and Togo. Fortunately Olympio received me and agreed to a meeting with the President of Ghana, provided that it take place on neutral ground in Dahomey.

At the Lagos Conference of the Monrovia Group (January, 1962) several heads of state questioned Nkrumah's policy of African hegemony, but this did not prevent a meeting several days later of the Foreign Ministers of Dahomey, Togo, and Ghana to prepare a summit conference of the three states. Several days later, however, Accra did a *volte-face*. One reason may have been that after the Lagos Conference, Olympio had proposed publicly a regional union of Dahomey, Togo, and Nigeria, to be based not only on economic ties but also on a common military defense, and this proposal to include Nigeria in an ensemble which excluded Ghana could not fail to irritate Nkrumah. Moreover, Nkrumah was apparently annoyed at the stubborn persistence of the Dahomean representatives, who sought at all costs to interest him in their own plans for economic development. By following one on the heels of another to Accra, the Dahomean ministers eroded Dahomey's position as an impartial arbiter. Hence, Accra proposed simply to invite President Olympio on an official visit to Ghana—during which the two parties would settle their differences directly. As might be expected, the Togolese chief of state could not accept such a procedure.

When Dahomey's attempt to end the Togo-Ghana conflict bogged down, other heads of state also tried to reach a compromise solution, above all to improve the domestic climate in Lomé. One morning in October, 1962, as I was traveling to the Ivory Coast to meet President Houphouet-Boigny, I found myself by chance next to Nicolas Grunitzky, then in exile in Dahomey, who was also traveling to Abidjan at the invitation of the Ivory Coast President. Houphouet-Boigny brought together almost all the exiled Togolese leaders from Ghana, Senegal, and Dahomey and came very close to settling the problem. But Olympio, who had grown suspicious and touchy, wrote that he preferred to see his adversaries return to Togo and make due apologies before being informed of the fate that would be reserved for them.

ASSASSINATION

Suddenly one day soon after, a commonplace affair of military gratuities, claimed by Togolese soldiers demobilized by the French Army, set off an explosion. On Sunday, January 13, 1963, the whole of Africa was awakened with the startling news that Olympio had been assassinated.

What had happened? It is not easy to say under what circumstances Sylvanus Olympio met his death that Sunday, shortly before he was scheduled to depart on an official visit to Monrovia.[1]

An emergency meeting of the Ministers of Foreign Affairs of the Monrovia Group was called in Lagos on January 24, 1963, at the initiative of the Nigerian government, which was inclined to suspect Ghana's intervention in the Togolese affair. At the opening session, Jaja Wachuku, then Minister of Foreign Affairs of Nigeria, raised two questions:

> Should automatic recognition be accorded to the provisional Government of Monsieur Grunitzky, without taking account of the suspension of the Constitution, of the dissolution of the Assembly, and of the abrogation of the electoral laws of the Republic of Togo? Can recognition be decided without taking account of the external influence and of the military constraint which contributed to bring to power and reinforce the new regime?

Two of Olympio's former ministers, Théophile Mally and Paulin Akouete, gave their version of the assassination and implicated both France and Ghana. In Mally's opinion, the assassination of President Olympio originated in events dating back to the elections of 1958, when the Togolese "nationalists" acceded to power. With regard to French officials, Mally stated in his document at the Lagos Conference:

> We point out that before the assassination of the President, the rebels warned Monsieur Maitrier, Commander of the Gendarmerie Nationale and Inspector of the Togolese Guard, by letter. In this letter it was stipulated that the French Ambassador in Togo had been advised, and, nevertheless, neither the French representative in Togo nor Commander Maitrier, Inspector of the Togolese Guard, saw fit to trouble themselves over the decision taken by the soldiers, and to inform the authorities. What is even more curious, the arms used to kill the President were taken from the military camp of Tokoin and distributed in the presence of Captain Bescond, the French officer responsible for this camp.[2]

The reading of this text could not leave the delegates indifferent. Even before calling in the Togolese representatives, the head of the Ivory Coast delegation, the Minister of State Auguste Denise, took the floor to warn his colleagues against accusations not specifically founded.

As soon as Mally's accusations were known in Paris, the Quai

---

[1] I have made personal inquiries concerning this incident. From all the accounts I obtained, the most plausible to my way of thinking is that of Gil Olympio, son of the late President, whose statement is contained in Appendix H, pp. 85–86.

[2] Gil Olympio has also expressed strong suspicions. If he does not make any specific accusations, he seriously doubts the good faith of certain foreigners in this episode.

d'Orsay published a particularly forceful denial, of which the press made great capital. It is perhaps worthwhile to translate what *Le Monde* on January 26, 1963, had to say:

> The first reactions of authorities in Paris to M. Mally's accusations against both the French Ambassador in Lomé and diverse French officers is one of indignation.
>
> Over against these allegations, termed "fanciful" and "slanderous," it is again recalled, as stated on January 13, that France had no part in the distressing events in Togo.
>
> On January 16, the Council of Ministers condemned the assassination of President Olympio, as well as all forms of violence in political affairs.
>
> Furthermore, it is pointed out that there are striking contradictions in remarks of the former Togolese Minister of the Interior, in that he links France and Ghana together in his imputations, while it is well known that when relations between Nkrumah and Olympio changed for the worse, France—at the request of Olympio—declared herself prepared to stand by the defense agreements linking her to Togo.

Nonetheless, Théophile Mally declared with great earnestness that the death of Sylvanus Olympio had not been an accident, that it had been premeditated by foreign forces. He delivered another indictment against Ghana, which, according to him, had utilized subversive methods. Thus, even before the 1958 elections, Nkrumah had supposedly bought off certain young Togolese partisans of the Juvento, by offering them bicycles and money. Back in 1959, Nkrumah had allegedly distributed important sums of money to several Togolese in order to lead them away from the policy of Olympio and to attempt to install the opposition party, favorable to his ideas, in power. Mally maintained that Nkrumah had introduced weapons into Togo. The first discovery of weapons had been in the home of Simon Kpodar. Fifty pistols and three thousand cartridges were found. Kpodar was to be arrested, but he fled and took refuge in Ghana. Antoine Meatchi, condemned to two years in prison for inciting a revolt during the elections of 1961, had escaped to join Kpodar in Accra.[3] Mally pointed out, further, that a few days prior to the assassination, the President of Ghana had addressed provocative letters to President Olympio; moreover, Ghanaian troops had been deployed all along the border between Togo and Ghana.

Dr. Vovor, representative of a provisional government which Grunitzky had installed, was more reserved. He stated:

> The death of President Olympio was an accidental death which surprised the entire population, for no one expected it. The brutal death is the deed of a small number of people . . . and not of the *population*.

---

[3]In reality, Meatchi had sought refuge principally in Abidjan, in the Ivory Coast.

Out of 700 soldiers demobilized by the French army, only a small number committed this atrocious crime.

For Dr. Vovor, the provisional government constituted "a lesser evil making it possible to avoid grave excesses."

After the Togolese had spoken, Emile Zinsou, Minister of Foreign Affairs of Dahomey, explained to the conference how the Togo-Ghana dispute had been followed in Cotonou and testified on the manner in which Grunitzky had accepted the presidency of the provisional government in Togo:

On Sunday, January 13, towards 6 A.M., President Maga was awakened by a telephone call from Lomé. The information given in this telephone call was so unexpected that the Dahomean Chief of State immediately called a meeting of the Council of Ministers, to whom he announced bluntly that a *coup d'état* had just been perpetrated in Togo and that President Sylvanus Olympio had been assassinated by mutinous soldiers.

Monsieur Grunitzky, former Prime Minister of Togo and a relative of Monsieur Olympio, was living in Cotonou.

When he received the news of the death of his brother-in-law, Grunitzky was deeply upset, and we saw him cry. After a moment of terror, of confusion, of anxiety, the Dahomean Ministers finally took a certain number of decisions.

It was decided that a mission would be sent to Togo, led by Monsieur Paul Darboux, and that another mission would go to Ghana, under the direction of Monsieur Zinsou.

When Monsieur Zinsou arrived at Dr. Nkrumah's, the latter thanked Dahomey for its action, and declared that he had first been informed of the *coup d'état* in Togo by a news bulletin of the Reuters Agency about 11 A.M. He added that, if he had not agreed politically with President Olympio, he nonetheless considered assassination as an act of cowardice having nothing to do with real political action. And Nkrumah added: "Whatever the point of view of observers, I am not at all involved in this affair."

Darboux had returned from Lomé and reported absolute calm. No one sought to take up the challenge of the soldiers. Dahomey decided that it did not have the right to "re-establish order" in Togo and that its intervention might, moreover, provoke the intervention of Ghana.

The first contacts with the rebels revealed that they had indeed meant to kill Olympio but that they had not thought out what should be done next, because they had no political ideas. They were almost all non-commissioned officers who sought in a frenzy someone to form a government, some thinking of Grunitzky, others of Meatchi. The Dahomean authorities informed Grunitzky of the situation, but his reply was, "Leave me in peace."

[47]

Finally, after considerable persuasion from other Togolese, Grunitzky agreed to leave for Lomé and to see on the spot whether he would try to form a new government. However, if there were no possibility of a national union, he said that he would definitely abandon the whole thing.

Minister Zinsou said that he had received a letter from Mally in which the latter asked him to enter into contact rapidly with certain influential people to tell them not to abandon Grunitzky, so that all should not be left in the hands of the rebels. It was under these circumstances, according to Zinsou, that Grunitzky agreed to return to power. When it was known that Grunitzky was the provisional President, "and not someone coming from Ghana," Zinsou added, "there seemed to be a general sigh of relief over the country. . . ."

Despite this account by the Minister from Dahomey, delegates from Sierra Leone, Nigeria, Upper Volta, and the Ivory Coast refused all suggestions of *de jure* or even *de facto* recognition of the Togolese provisional government. Auguste Denise demanded that a mission be dispatched to Togo to attempt to uncover what had happened, what the reasons behind it were, and who were the instigators. He suspected that the subversive plot was the work of intellectuals who sent stooges to do their dirty work for them and who had intended to invite Meatchi, the former Minister of Agriculture, to assume power. He added that the attitude of the Ivory Coast was dictated, above all, by the ties which seemed to exist between the outbreak of the *coup d'état* in Togo and the discovery of a plot in Abidjan. In many circles, a case was made of the friendship between the former Minister of Health of the Ivory Coast, Amadou Kone, condemned to death for conspiracy, and Meatchi, who, during his exile, often chose to live at the home of Dr. Kone, who, furthermore, as a favor, had offered to Mme Meatchi (Josephine Bayor) a position as a nurse in Abidjan. The Minister from Upper Volta, for his part, supported the Ivory Coast delegate vigorously in his refusal to recognize the Grunitzky government. He emphasized the fact that Dr. Vovor, representing Grunitzky, had declared that the rebellion was not the work of the population but the deed of a handful of men.

The arguments developed by the delegates from Sierra Leone and Nigeria were more concerned with the legal aspects of the problem and, above all, with the fact that the Togolese constitution provided for cases of a vacancy in office. What was called for, therefore, they asserted, was to rely on the regular organs first, rather than recognizing purely and simply a government installed by force.

Two other lines of argument differed fundamentally from those just mentioned. Senegal was one of the very few states that had recognized the Grunitzky provisional government, several days after its hasty recognition by Ghana.[4] Senegal's condemnation of the assassination was categorical, but, according to the Senegalese minister, it was a question of an internal Togolese issue. Now, since the new government gave representation to all the political forces of the country and included a member of the party of the late President Olympio, Senegal recognized it in the hope that it would expedite the solution of the problems posed by the political vacuum created in this brother country.

Foreign Minister Betayene of the Federal Republic of Cameroon, probably one of the most practical men at the conference, requested of his colleagues that they avoid positions which would only weaken the authority of the Monrovia Group. He pointed out that the recognition of one state by another was a problem to be left to the discretion of each government, that a wide range of considerations (proximity, economic interests, political interests, struggles for influence, etc.) came into play in the motives determining the decision of such and such a country.

It was this point of view, strongly supported by Minister Zinsou and the delegate from Senegal, that finally won out. The conference adopted a resolution deploring the assassination of Sylvanus Olympio, recommending that member states come to the aid of the family of the deceased, and insisting on the initiation of procedures aimed at a return to republican legality in Togo. A special commission was constituted to meet with Grunitzky and to inform him of the point of view of the Lagos Conference.

AFTERMATH

The Lagos Conference provoked varied reactions. After the numerous accusations made against her during the meetings, Ghana could not remain indifferent, thus confirming by her silence all the very harsh suspicions still in the air. Ambassador Doe, the Ghanaian High Commissioner in Nigeria, published on January 26, 1963, in the name of his government, a declaration in which he rejected the allegations that Olympio's assassination had been planned in Ghana. Ambassador Doe emphasized that the Togolese military junta had itself claimed the responsibility for this assassination. As to the fact that Meatchi had taken refuge in Accra, the High Commissioner queried: "Why not accuse Dahomey on the same grounds as Ghana for having offered asylum to Grunitzky?" Replying to those who reproached Nkrumah for having recognized the Togolese provisional government too hastily, Ambassador Doe pointed out that until the elaboration of a common foreign policy in the framework

---

[4]Grunitzky had been a member of the IOM (Indépendants d'Outre-Mer) group in the French Parliament—the party to which Senghor belonged.

of African unity, Ghana had the sovereign right to recognize whatever government it pleased.

Grunitzky's problems, however, had not ended. During the Conference of the UAM in Ouagadougou, he addressed a memorandum to the heads of state. After deploring the tragic death of Olympio, he nonetheless invited the African heads of state to face the situation in Togo "with *sang froid* and understanding." The memorandum set out the conditions under which the provisional government had been formed in order to prevent the growth of anarchy, and it pointed to a number of measures taken by the provisional government to restore order and civil liberties. The memorandum strongly affirmed that "No military junta exists in Togo."

Finally, the memorandum stated that except for Liberia and Guinea, which had recalled their ambassadors, all the other countries that had entered into diplomatic relations with Togo (France, Great Britain, U.S.A., West Germany, U.S.S.R., Israel) had maintained their representatives. As for Ghana, Grunitzky stated: "It was not up to the Provisional Government that Ghana should be the first country to recognize its existence officially. . . . In fact, at the present time, the attitude of the Ghanaian government toward Togo stills seems difficult to define. The Provisional Government has noticed recently with surprise an uninterrupted line of barbed wire along the border . . ., and the passage of vehicles and individuals also still remains difficult." In conclusion, the Grunitzky government discreetly reaffirmed its sympathy for the UAM and hoped that the states of this organization would recognize it.

The debate on the Togolese affair in Ouagadougou was very lively. Despite the forceful dialectic of Senghor and Ahidjo, Houphouet-Boigny and Yameogo put a stop to the recognition of the Togolese government, invoking the same reasons that their delegates had already developed during the Lagos Conference. In the end, it was decided to leave to the President of Dahomey the task of following the Togolese situation and of informing his colleagues, who, in the light of his information, could eventually decide about recognizing the Grunitzky government.

After elections in which Grunitzky was elected President, Meatchi Vice President, and a new Parliament was installed, the new government had hoped to be present at the Pan-African Conference of Addis Ababa in May, 1963, but Nigeria, the Ivory Coast, and especially Guinea continued to treat it with great reserve. Nonetheless, some weeks later, all the African states recognized that the Togolese people had freely pronounced in favor of reconciliation, and the Grunitzky government was finally admitted at its request as the fourteenth member of the UAM.

VI

Sequel and Conclusion

DISSOLUTION

In the period since the events analyzed in the preceding chapters, the political situation in Africa has changed so radically that the leaders of the UAM have had to question the survival of their "club."

The most significant event was the Conference of Addis Ababa, which turned into a grand reconciliation rite, where all factions solemnly swore that the divisions of yesterday must come to an end and where in the midst of a general euphoria the Organization for African Unity (OAU) was created. After subscribing to the charter of the new organization, the leaders of the UAM met in Cotonou in July, 1963, to draw the logical conclusions for their own organization. A great debate began there between the Abolitionists and the Conservatives. A more immediate issue arose, however.

My successor at the UAM Secretariat, Bertrand Dagnon, had been killed in a crash five weeks after assuming office. Several heads of state thought that after three Dahomeans it was time for a change. Many looked to the Deputy Secretary-General, Germain Mba, from Gabon. In a telegram to President Maga, President Mba of Gabon in fact strongly protested against "the Dahomean dynasty of Secretaries-General of the UAM," and he abstained from the conference in Cotonou. But Maga made the issue a personal one and pleaded, begged, and threatened. He finally succeeded in getting his candidate, Max Zollner, then Counselor to the Dahomean Delegation at the UN, appointed.

That such problems should plague the UAM at the Cotonou Conference was unfortunate, for more important things were at stake. The unpredictable UAM President in office at the time, Maurice Yameogo, had in mind to appoint the Secretary-General of Maga's choice and, at the same time, to obtain dissolution of the Union! No such decision was made at Cotonou, but the handwriting was on the wall when the UAM heads of state met next, in March, 1964, in Dakar. At the Dakar Conference, the postponed conclusions were made clear:

(1) the UAM was dissolved as a political organization;

(2) the UAMCE (Union Africaine et Malgache de Coopération

Economique) was formed to supplant the OAMCE and continue purely technical exchanges and assistance;

(3) the Secretariat of this only remaining formal link was stationed at Yaoundé (whereas UAM headquarters had been at Cotonou);

(4) a citizen of Senegal was appointed to head the new Secretariat.

REGROUPING

These decisions taken in Dakar aroused distrust in Abidjan. During the spring of 1964, President Senghor was very prominent in African politics. President Grunitzky was consolidating his position in Togo, and it must not be forgotten that Grunitzky had formerly belonged to Senghor's party at the Palais Bourbon, the Indépendants d'Outre-Mer. In Dahomey, President Houphouet-Boigny's faithful ally, Maga, was overthrown. The new leaders (Apithy and Ahomadegbé) deliberately drifted away from Abidjan and toward Dakar. In Cameroon, President Ahidjo, still another Indépendant d'Outre-Mer, continued to look to Senghor and had just made an official visit to Senegal. In Gabon, Aubame, one of the Senegalese leader's best friends, had just missed coming to power, and Houphouet-Boigny's ally Leon Mba was losing ground.

It was at that point that Houphouet-Boigny pulled up short. Yameogo, his faithful spokesman for some time—who had preached the dissolution of the UAM at Cotonou and supported all the decisions taken at Dakar—decided to reconsider his position. He proclaimed that the UAM should be re-established and that political relations among the French-speaking states were more important than economic relations. France, it is true, had not much appreciated the transformation of the UAM into the UAMCE and had perhaps advised maintaining the former ties.

The ensuing conference at Nouakchott, Mauritania, in March, 1965, was quite a spectacle. In order to preserve the unity of the French-speaking group, the OCAM (African and Malagasy Common Organization) was formed to serve as a forum for the former members of the UAM. But simultaneously with the OCAM, an old conflict reappeared on the horizon—the Congo crisis. Tshombe, the former separatist leader of Katanga, became Prime Minister of the central government, and this event once again left Africa deeply divided.

On the other hand, there were those who, even though personally partial to Tshombe, refused to play the game of subversive activity. For them, to allow the Congolese rebels to destroy the government of Leopoldville was to encourage criminal and subversive tactics, allegedly brought into Africa by China through Ghana and perhaps Guinea. Diverse accusations were made against Nkrumah, and there were bitter exchanges between Sékou Touré, Yameogo, and Houphouet-Boigny. It was essentially for reasons of domestic political equilibrium and to avoid the counter-implications of subversion that the majority of the leaders of the OCAM decided to accord their protection to Tshombe, as representative of the Leopoldville government.

Other leaders, however, refused to follow this course. President Moktar Ould Daddah of Mauritania, also acting President of the OCAM, refused from the beginning. Then Presidents Ahidjo of Cameroon and Massamba-Débat of Congo-Brazzaville took the same position. Their arguments may be summed up as follows.

First, internal subversion raises the question of the structure of a state—if a truly democratic means of opposition is open, subversion will be limited and perhaps firmly controlled. If there is dictatorship, under any label, and there is no other means of ending it, the road is open to subversive activity.

Second, it must not be forgotten that the Congo is divided between two authorities, which henceforth must both be taken into account: the "legitimate" government in Leopoldville and a diffused revolutionary authority, which not only sparked the present revolt extending across the whole country but is also one of the parties in the continuing Congolese civil war. A government which, despite massive foreign assistance, is incapable of maintaining order and security on its territory is no longer a national government.

Third, it is important to recall that Africa's two most basic principles are at stake in the Congo—dignity in the face of systematic racism, and solidarity across national lines. The mercenaries fighting the rebels in the Congo are the very South Africans and Portuguese who categorically refuse to acknowledge the new world coming into being in Africa.

Fourth, the opposite camps must be brought to the negotiating table. But no side will negotiate when it has the impression of being the stronger, when it thinks it can crush its adversary. Leopoldville will not agree to negotiations so long as it receives massive foreign military support and can thereby hope for complete victory. It will be difficult to convince the "rebels" to negotiate so long as they are armed to the teeth from abroad and given the possibility of a Castro-style victory.

These were the arguments, but there was no opportunity to discuss them. Moktar Ould Daddah, Ahidjo, and Massamba-Débat refused to attend the meeting scheduled to debate the admission of the Congo to the OCAM.

Houphouet-Boigny, resuming leadership of the Brazzaville Group after the Nouakchott Conference and benefiting from Senghor's neutrality, thereupon assumed the responsibility of integrating the Congo into the French-speaking club and of embracing Tshombe as the Prime Minister of a brother state. Constitutionally, nothing barred him,

[53]

since the OCAM has no charter, and so at a conference at Abidjan, not attended by all member states, Congo-Leopoldville, represented by Tshombe, was taken into the organization. Politically, however, this act was divisive.

Moktar Ould Daddah, who made no secret of his preference for the OAU, had been requested to resign from the Presidency of the OCAM, and the meeting at Abidjan was held without him. Consequently, he withdrew Mauritania from the organization entirely after the admission of the Tshombe government. Now Cameroon is tending toward the same position. In a speech delivered at Douala on July 9, 1965, President Ahidjo stated: "If the progress of the OCAM continues in its present direction, I do not see how Cameroon can maintain its membership for long."

With Mauritania, Cameroon, and Congo-Brazzaville in opposition, with the OAU attracting Pan-African sentiment, at least for the present, and with rivalry between Senghor and Houphouet-Boigny, the future of the OCAM is doubtful. Still more doubtful is a revival of the UAM. But the need for African unity remains.

A Basis for Continental Action

After discussing the actual working of the organization and considering recent developments, it seems appropriate to draw some conclusions about the UAM's place in the over-all Pan-African picture. First, in a new way an old lesson has been demonstrated: the conditions necessary for African development do not exist within the framework of micro-nations. Second, the best prospects for Pan-Africanism may not coincide with linguistic zones.

I strongly believe that it would be a mistake to divide Africa into compartments like "French-speaking" and "English-speaking." Either these "clubs" must form truly federated states, or their cooperation will come to nothing, isolated from the Pan-African context.. "Clubs" run the risk of perpetuating the former dependence. As Renan said, "What makes a nation *is not simply to speak the same language* . . . but to have undertaken great things together in the past and to aspire to do so again in the future." This definition of the nation applies quite well to a country like Switzerland, which, despite its variety of languages, religions, and economic pursuits, stands at the crossroads of world events. The importance of the Federal Republic of Cameroon also deserves to be emphasized as an example of a multilingual state.

If one casts a glance at the background and the ideas of the men who will build tomorrow's Africa, it is clear that the future cannot be a mere continuation of the present. The men who formed the UAM and who participate in the OCAM today were all either French

[54]

deputies or their direct heirs. Their political horizon was colored by the Palais Bourbon, the Cross of Lorraine, the Grand Councils of the AOF and AEF, etc. Political life for them is inseparable from France.

Things will not be the same for those studying at the Sorbonne or in other French universities today. Today's students are not only emancipated—they are free men with open minds. Even if growing age and experience of the facts of life were to temper their zeal, it is certain that they will not believe in a French-speaking Africa. They have no *political* ties to France. What they do owe to France is a universal culture—which, indeed, most of their elders did not receive to the same extent. The Africa of their conception is a grown-up Africa, turned toward universals in a mature world. With this perspective of the world, they are making contacts in Paris that today's governments decline.

It is certain, for instance, that in recognizing the Peoples' Republic of China, France took the most decisive step in the history of African political development. It is indeed more important for Peking to be represented in Paris than in Ouagadougou. It is in Paris that contacts between tomorrow's Africa and China will be multiplied and consolidated. It is in Paris that the idea of a Revolutionary Africa will finally reach the Continent through its future statesmen. The interests of France, of China, and of that new Africa remain to be determined. This will not be an easy task. Other contacts are also being made— in the Soviet Union, in the United States, in Scandinavia, etc. Ten years from now, the African elite will truly represent a cross-section of the world. I am convinced that it is not in the interest of France to maintain a group of African states with numerous and complicated problems as a sort of new colonial empire.

It seems also useful to stress at this point the South African question and to recall that many African leaders (even the most moderate) are more and more disturbed and bitter when it appears to them that some Western powers (Great Britain and France included) are quite willingly supporting the Verwoerd regime. These Western powers are helping the South African government to build military and police power and to resist any political or economic pressure. There is indeed a sad and tragic contradiction in acting for decolonization here and there while at the same time strongly encouraging apartheid and exploitation somewhere else in the same continent. A showdown might come sooner or later involving both political and economic interests of Eastern and Western countries and leading to some hot tension—even a local military conflict—unless a new policy is quickly undertaken.

What Africa awaits from France is a broadening of the political spectrum. Moreover, the way has been opened. Relations between the Paris government and the English-speaking countries of Africa are

[55]

growing. Michel Habib Deloncle, French Secretary of State for Foreign Affairs, has undertaken in the name of General de Gaulle the establishing of ties with Kenya, Tanzania, Sierra Leone, and Nigeria. There has also been a growing rapprochement with Ghana. The future of France in Africa and the future of the Pan-African ideal may one day coincide, eliminating the strategic necessity of a French-speaking group that resembles a missionary field or an overseas territory. A federation associating wholly or partially Ghana, Togo, Dahomey, and Nigeria, for instance, could also be in the interest of France—and I do not think Paris would be opposed if the parties concerned were to decide to bring about in fact what reason and economics seem to dictate. This example points up the possibility of complementary regional regroupings capable of laying the basic foundations necessary to organizations for African unity.

These regional regroupings would seem useful. To pretend that the entire continent could achieve unity here and now, without gradual adjustments, is to opt in favor of an illusory universalism which leaves each state free to continue its present "sovereign" status whenever there is lack of agreement at the continental level, which will nearly always be the case.

I certainly have the greatest sympathy for the Pan-African ideas of President Kwame Nkrumah, who seems to me absolutely right in his "crusade for unity." I do not believe, however, in an Africa united on a continental level under a single government. This ambition overlooks one important factor, to my way of thinking. Governments owe their existence and effectiveness to several basic factors—and among them, the possibility of quickly reaching the entire territory constituting the state. Even with all the modern means of communication available, this condition appears to me difficult, if not impossible, in the case of a government of the whole African continent.

Africa is comparable in size to more than the United States, Canada, China, and India together. To govern such an area from one capital seems to me a titanic undertaking—and Africans are not Titans any more than other men.

But of the five continents, Africa at present contains the greatest number of states—nearly 40, with perhaps more to come. Between this mosaic of Lilliputian states and the gigantic proportions of a single continental government, there surely lies room for effective, reasonable, and human solutions. Instead of 40 states, we could surely envisage 10 or even 5 perfectly viable federations. For this reason, it would seem wise for the African states to start out on this constructive path resolutely and prudently, consulting with one another increasingly and, above all, refusing systematically to be influenced by the interests, however understandable they may be, of the former colonizers.

But Africa's problems are not limited to geography, economy, and

[56]

language. Ideological divisions are appearing in Africa increasingly, especially various conceptions of an ill-defined but widely proclaimed "socialism." It will not be easy to unite states that have set out in different directions—short of working to coordinate those movements and to render the divergences less sharp. Research will be indispensable here to arrive at a clear definition of the state, the economy, democracy, social organization. Pan-Africanism requires clear thinking.

Numerous observers have wondered what role foreign powers and national and international organizations for aid and development might play in African unification. Many are of the opinion that it would be in the definite interest of Africa and the world if technical assistance were given not to individual states but to groups of states joined together geographically, economically, and even politically. But, as Joseph Nye has pointed out, a process of unity imposed from without would too much resemble the colonial period, when wide regions were formed at the metropole's will.[1] Such a process would seem touchy and difficult today, and the immediate political interests of the former metropoles do not always coincide with the formation and consolidation of broader economic and political groupings in Africa.

It is up to the Africans to take the initiative. There may be fear that some of the initiatives will lead to violence. But it is obvious that enclaves like Gambia will either follow the lead of Zanzibar, integrated in Tanganyika, or else risk provoking scenes like the *fait accompli* in Goa. This said, wider federations will be the fruit of the determination of African leaders, free from the flimsy trappings of protocol, of national flags, of official visits, of brassy military reviews, of a seat at the UN. If Africans demonstrate such a determination, it is not impossible that organizations for economic cooperation and for development assistance may make a decisive contribution to saving a continent in tatters.

Given, then, that the Brazzaville, Monrovia, and Casablanca Groups ought no longer to exist as such, it is appropriate to proceed to a more rational reorganization within the framework of the OAU. To that end, it would be desirable: for an effective secretariat to be set up for the whole continent (staffed by technically competent personnel with all modern means of communication and administration at their disposal); for intermediate-level regional organizations (freely conceived and accepted by both their founders and beneficiaries) to be set up, in harmony with geographic, economic, ethnic, and cultural realities.

These intermediate structures would form, at least temporarily, the basis for continental action. In order to assure that they do not

---

[1]Nye, "Patterns and Catalysts in Regional Integration," *International Organization*, Vol. XIX, No. 4 (Autumn, 1965).

serve to resurrect the rivalries of the former groups, these basic regional organizations should be quite tightly joined together at the top, not only through legal and administrative documents but also through specifically designated coordinating agents who would be regional secretaries of the OAU. For example, there might be regional unions in North, South, East, West, and Central Africa. Each regional union would coordinate the administrative, economic, and military services of its own geographic zone, on the condition that this zone be an integral part of the OAU.

It is important to note that, at the initiative of Robert Gardiner, the United Nations Economic Commission for Africa has already developed a framework corresponding to these conclusions. The Commission, indeed, outlines four sub-regions: a Northern sub-region with headquarters in Tangiers; a Western sub-region with headquarters in Niamey; a Central sub-region with headquarters in Leopoldville; an Eastern sub-region with headquarters in Lusaka. If other international organizations were to follow this model, and if the OAU were likewise to adopt it, a great step would be taken toward improved cooperation that one day might result in federation.

Four regional groupings, intelligently conceived and *freely accepted*, would already qualify as potential federations within the wider African confederation. This would limit to some extent the havoc wrought by the demon of balkanization, which all African leaders denounce with lyrical elegance in their speeches while secretly blessing it for having given them the opportunity of a seat in the UN, a flag, a national anthem, and the privilege of making official visits to all the great capitals of the world.

I strongly believe that governments alone cannot build Africa and that the future of Pan-Africanism does not depend solely on their will. I would go so far as to maintain that governments, which are defined by the attributes of sovereignty, constitute the most serious obstacle to unity. The force and motivation must be sought elsewhere. For my part, I look to the peoples of Africa. I find encouragement in the lucidity and courage of the students, in the struggle of the workers and labor unions against collective poverty, in the education of women —their *prise de conscience,* their organizations, their unique role in the construction of multinational societies.

The governments will follow and, finding encouragement, will realize in spite of themselves the desired miracle. I shall explain myself more specifically in summing up as follows.

The miracle of African unity depends on the combined efforts of both domestic and international agents of federation: on the combined efforts of the governments, labor unions, students, and women of Africa —but also, and to almost as great an extent, on the action of international organizations both regional and global in scope and on the policy of industrialized countries, whose economic aid has been inefficiently dispersed for political reasons. Should this aid be coordinated, it would very likely promote reorganization in Africa. Then the votes in the UN would be truly democratic, corresponding to more or less parallel realities, and permitting equal partners to cooperate effectively.

This prospect would likewise pave the way for a closer African collaboration with the regional offices of international organizations, in solving the numerous technical problems which these organizations of cooperation are particularly well equipped to handle. There would thus no longer be any temptation to put together a host of short-lived organizations, difficult to manage because of the lack of qualified personnel and inadequate budgets.

Outsiders often point out, quite rightly, that there are too many organizations in Africa. These organizations, furthermore, are not content to sit back and administer some given general policy; they are also involved in problems of technical cooperation. And so there ensues a proliferation of cultural commissions, scientific commissions, economic commissions, secretariats for telecommunications, etc.

If Africa were to be restructured harmoniously within the framework of the OAU—with apparatus only for general administration, for political studies, and for the execution of the major decisions of the heads of state—then all problems of a technical nature could be entrusted to a few international organizations capable of coordinating the means available: that is, endowed with the administrative personnel, the necessary experts, and adequate financial means. Thus, more confidence should be placed in the United Nations Economic Commission for Africa. And, for instance, the Regional Office of the World Health Organization in Brazzaville should receive strong support from the OAU because certain of their objectives are the same. The International Union of Telecommunications should be asked to set up a Central Office, to foster the expansion of telecommunications on the African continent and to replace the score of small secretariats, which, however useful, are surely more expensive and inefficient to maintain.

The International Labour Office might also play a prime role. In his Introduction to my book, *La formation des cadres africains en vue de la croissance économique* (Paris: Diloutremer, 1965) Alfred Sauvy emphasizes this point. The following passage, translated into English, represents his views:

A country behind the times at the moment—prey to the pressure of the great powers and to poverty—will not be politically independent until the day when it can utilize its own natural resources efficiently and intensively and satisfy its principal needs. . . . When the people of a country in Asia, Africa, or Latin America are prepared *to manage their resources by themselves,* financial problems will diminish in intensity.

Along with Sauvy, I am convinced that African economic development will be achieved primarily by the workers. These workers are very much in need of solid labor unions. They need an organization of their own and ties to the other workers of the world. I am certain that they do not wish to see the process of economic growth lead to the defeat of what Nasser has so rightly described as: "A methodical African mind and a dynamic African nerve." The Egyptian President is not alone in recognizing so clearly the realities of today and tomorrow. Senghor, Sékou Touré, and Modibo Keita know and have stated with great conviction that the morale of the workers is the true key to the problem of development.

Neo-colonialism in the countries of the UAM cannot be blamed entirely on Paris. The same France which subjects Chad or Niger to vassalization through its aid programs (cf. Chap. I) cooperates quite well with socialists, Arabs, and revolutionary Algeria. The same France which sends its paratroopers to impose political order in Gabon is also the France that cooperates willingly with Communist China, seeks ties with Hungary and Rumania, and is capable of a rapprochement with the Soviet Union and Egypt. It is the same France that aspires in Europe to be the artisan of a new political order capable of checking what she considers to be the preponderance of United States policy.

It is thus up to the former members of the UAM to define their purposes more precisely, to join forces with their neighbors and work out more fertile and complete areas of cooperation.

For it is certain that an Africa so organized, reconciled unto itself, accepting a rigorous discipline to free itself of its various servitudes, mindful that the key to its problems lies not in a "grandeur" which leads to isolation but in a harmony that unites—no matter what language this Africa speaks, no nation will hesitate to cooperate with it. This Africa will surely merit the respect of the world.

A

Charter of the Union Africaine et Malgache[1]

Article 1

The Union Africaine et Malgache is a union of independent and sovereign States, open to any independent African State.

Admission of a State to the UAM shall be decided by the unanimous vote of the members of the Union.

Article 2

The UAM is founded on the solidarity uniting its members.

Its goal is to organize the cooperation of its members in all domains of foreign policy, in order to reinforce their solidarity, to assure their collective security, to foster their economic development, to maintain peace in Africa, in Malagasy, and in the world.

Article 3

The UAM shall have a General Administrative Secretariat, with headquarters at Cotonou. The Administrative Secretary-General shall be appointed for two years by the Conference of Heads of State and Government, upon proposal of the President of the Republic of Dahomey. His salary shall be established by the same Conference, which also shall approve the annual budget of the General Administrative Secretariat. Each State's contribution to that budget shall be proportional to the operating budget of each member State.

Article 4

The general policy of the UAM shall be defined by the Conference of the Heads of State and Government, which shall meet in ordinary session twice annually. Extraordinary sessions may be called at the initiative of any State, supported by a majority of the members of the Union.

Between these sessions, according to the nature of the problems, meetings of the appropriate ministers, experts, or permanent United Nations delegates will be held.

Motions shall be carried by a simple majority vote. Discipline shall be obligatory in questions concerning decolonization.

Article 5

A UAM Group shall be formed at the United Nations.

This Group shall hold compulsory meetings to concert action before all important decisions.

Article 6

The present Charter shall be published in the Official Record of each member State.

TANANARIVE, SEPTEMBER 12, 1961

---

[1]All the documents appended to this paper have been translated.

B

Relations among the Secretariats

The relationship of secretariats to each other within the UAM was initially confused. Without consideration of possible ties and division of responsibilities and authority among them, they were created by separate agreements, discussed below.

The OAMCE

Article 2 of the treaty instituting the OAMCE reads: "The Organization aims at progressive rapprochement of the economic policies of the member States and the coordination of their development planning." This treaty authorized a Council to define the general policy of the Organization. Each State was represented by one delegate to this Council, at ministerial rank or below, and the Council was to elect its President at each session from among the delegates.

As stated in Article 15 of the treaty, "The Council is assisted in its task by a Secretary-General it names for two years." According to Article 16, "Under the authority of the Council, the Secretary-General directs the functioning of the Organization."

The UAMPT

The covenant establishing the UAMPT lays down as the Organization's role "to promote, maintain, and extend coordination and cooperation among its members for the amelioration and rational organization of postal and telecommunications" (Art. 2). Articles 4-5 stipulate that the UAM Committee of Ministers shall name the UAMPT Secretary-General, who, as head of a "technical and administrative organ of permanent character," is "placed under the direct authority of the President of the Committee of Ministers."

The UAMD

Article 11 of the defense pact declares that general defense policy "shall be decided at the Conference of the Heads of State." Article 12 authorizes a UAMD Council "where each member State shall be represented by one delegate plenipotentiary." Article 13 creates a secretariat "at the service of the Council, for the purpose of assuring the continuity of its work as well as preparing its sessions."

The Dakar Protocol

In the spirit of the agreements cited above, Presidents Ahidjo and Mba attempted to give some structure to the relations among the Secretaries-General. After a series of letters, the following Protocol was adopted at Dakar in November, 1962:

The Heads of State and Government of the member countries of the Union Africaine et Malgache,

Considering the UAM Charter signed in Tananarive, September 12, 1961,

Considering the treaties, pacts, conventions, and agreements within the UAM . . . ,

Do agree to the following relations among the diverse Organizations created for the purpose of cooperation among the member states of the Union:

Article 1

The Conference of the Heads of State and Government of the member states of the UAM shall be the highest instance of the Union.

The President of the UAM shall be permanently assisted by the Administrative Secretary-General.

Article 2

The Specialized Organizations of the UAM are:

—the African and Malagasy Organization for Economic Cooperation;

—the African and Malagasy Defense Union;

—the African and Malagasy Union for Postal and Telecommunications.

Article 3

The highest instance of each Specialized Organization shall be a Council of Ministers or Plenipotentiaries. This Council shall propose measures taken on its level to the Conference of Heads of State and Government for approbation.

This Council shall have at its disposal a General Secretariat whose headquarters shall be at:

Yaoundé for the OAMCE;

Ouagadougou for the UAMD;

Brazzaville for the UAMPT.

Article 4

The General Secretariat of each Organization shall be accountable to the President of the Council of that Organization.

The Secretary-General of each Organization shall draw up, or have drawn up by committees or commissions of experts, plans or proposals for decisions, resolutions, or recommendations within his particular jurisdiction, for submission to the Council, before presentation to the Conference of Heads of State and Government.

He shall assist the President of the Council during the presentation of these plans and proposals to the Conference of the Heads of State and Government.

Article 5

There shall be one budget for the whole UAM, and the President in office shall be the *Ordonnateur principal.*

[63]

The Secretaries-General are personally responsible for the disposition of the credits accorded to them.

The rules for the preparation, execution, and control of the UAM budget shall form the subject of a separate text.

Article 6

Within the framework of the directives with which he shall be charged, the Administrative Secretary-General shall be charged with the formulation of proposals for decisions, resolutions, and recommendations for the Conference of Heads of State and Government.

He shall take charge of the Secretariat at the Conference of the Heads of State and Government.

He shall preside over the execution of decisions, resolutions, and recommendations of the Conference of Heads of State and Government and shall be kept informed by the Secretaries-General of the Specialized Organizations of their respective activities.

Article 7

Acceptance of the Charter of the UAM automatically implies adherence to the Specialized Organizations.

However, in the case of the UAMD, this acceptance may be made subject to special conditions.

Article 8

The present Protocol shall enter into force upon its adoption by the States.

Despite this effort at clarification, tensions remained in relations among the Secretaries-General until the elimination of separate secretariats and the creation of the UAMCE with a single Secretary-General. Because of its commercial and relatively autonomous status, as well as the fact that Malagasy is not a member, Air Afrique has been left out of this account. Relations between Air Afrique and the UAM Administrative Secretariat, however, were excellent.

C

Finances of the UAM

TABLE 1

TOTAL ADMINISTRATIVE AND INVESTMENT BUDGET

	1962		1963	
Administrative Secretariat				
Personnel	22,620,000	francs CFA	27,124,000	francs CFA
Supplies and Services	15,030,000		12,500,000	
Transportation	10,000,000		10,000,000	
Rent	5,160,000		3,000,000	
Equipment	5,500,000		2,000,000	
Emergency Fund	—		2,000,000	
New York Office	—		26,000,000	
		58,310,000		82,624,000
OAMCE Secretariat				
Personnel	22,620,000		23,044,000	
Supplies	6,700,000		7,500,000	
Transportation	10,000,000		10,000,000	
Rent	5,160,000		6,800,000	
Equipment	5,500,000		1,500,000	
		49,980,000		48,844,000
UAMPT Secretariat				
Personnel	10,080,000		16,652,000	
Supplies	3,600,000		3,500,000	
Transportation	2,000,000		5,000,000	
Rent	3,360,000		7,380,000	
Equipment	3,400,000		1,500,000	
		22,440,000		34,032,000
UAMD Secretariat				
Personnel	10,080,000		29,024,000	
Supplies	3,600,000		6,000,000	
Transportation	2,000,000		7,000,000	
Rent	3,360,000		12,700,000	
Equipment	3,400,000		5,000,000	
		22,440,000		59,724,000
Investment Expenditures				
Administrative Secretariat	—		29,000,000	
OAMCE Secretariat	—		30,000,000	
				59,000,000
Total		153,170,000 francs CFA		284,224,000 francs CFA

Table 2

Proportional Assessment of 12 UAM Members for
4 Common Budgets, 1962

(Francs CFA)

	Secretariat*	OAMCE	UAMPT	UAMD	Total	%
Cameroon	6,123,000	6,123,000	2,749,000	2,749,000	17,744,000	12.25
Central African Republic	1,499,000	1,499,000	673,000	673,000	4,344,000	3
Congo-Brazzaville	2,249,000	2,249,000	1,010,000	1,010,000	6,518,000	4.5
Ivory Coast	8,247,000	8,247,000	3,703,000	3,703,000	23,900,000	16.5
Dahomey	2,999,000	2,999,000	1,346,000	1,346,000	8,690,000	6
Gabon	1,999,000	1,999,000	898,000	898,000	5,794,000	4
Malagasy	7,997,000	7,997,000	3,591,000	3,591,000	23,176,000	16
Mauritania	1,499,000	1,499,000	673,000	673,000	4,344,000	3
Niger	2,874,000	2,874,000	1,290,000	1,290,000	8,328,000	5.75
Senegal	9,121,000	9,121,000	4,095,000	4,095,000	26,432,000	18.25
Chad	2,374,000	2,374,000	1,066,000	1,066,000	6,880,000	4.75
Upper Volta	2,999,000	2,999,000	1,346,000	1,346,000	8,690,000	6
Total	49,980,000	49,980,000	22,440,000	22,440,000	144,840,000	100 %

*Some states contributed funds over and above their assessed share, as reflected in Table 1.

D

Conferences of the Heads of State

Place	Date	Heads of State and Government		Agenda	Major Decisions	Miscellaneous Observations
		Present	Absent			
1. Abidjan	25–26 October 1960	Ahidjo (Cameroon)	Mba (Gabon), represented by Migolet, Labor Minister	Algerian War	Support Mauritanian independence against Moroccan ambitions	Presiding: Houphouet-Boigny
		Youlou (Congo-Brazzaville)		Independence of Mauritania and difficulties with Morocco		
		Houphouet-Boigny (Ivory Coast)	Dacko (Central African Republic), represented by Bandio, Minister of the Interior	Problems of the Congo-Leopoldville	Favor direct negotiations between France and Algeria without recourse to UN	Tsiranana (Malagasy) was not present; he was on an official visit to Paris
		Maga (Dahomey)				
		Yameogo (Upper Volta)		Project of creating bonds among French-speaking states		The delegate from Chad did not arrive in time to take part in the meetings
		Ould Daddah (Mauritania)			Promote regular meetings between French-speaking states	
		Hamani Diori (Niger)				
		Senghor (Senegal)				

Place	Date	Heads of State and Government		Agenda	Major Decisions	Miscellaneous Observations
		Present	Absent			
2. Brazzaville	15–19 December 1960	Ahidjo Youlou Houphouet-Boigny Dacko Maga Yameogo Tsiranana Ould Daddah Hamani Diori Senghor and Dia Tombalbaye (Chad)	None	Algerian War Congo question Organization of French-speaking states Relations among states	Clear position against UN intervention in Algeria Encouraging a round-table conference of Congolese leaders	Presiding: Houphouet-Boigny The Congo-Leopoldville sent 18 observers, among them: Kasavubu Tshombe Bomboko

3. Yaoundé	26–28 March 1961	Ahidjo Youlou Houphouet-Boigny Dacko Maga Mba Yameogo Tsiranana Ould Daddah Hamani Diori Senghor and Dia Tombalbaye	None	Inter-state relations	Creation of OAMCE Creation of Air Afrique	Presiding: Tsiranana

[69]

Place	Date	Heads of State and Government		Agenda	Major Decisions	Miscellaneous Observations
		Present	Absent			
4. Tananarive	4–12 September 1961	Ahidjo Youlou Maga Mba Yameogo Tsiranana Ould Daddah Hamani Diori Senghor Tombalbaye	Houphouet-Boigny, represented by Yacé, President of Ivory Coast National Assembly Dacko, represented by Dejean, Minister of Foreign Affairs	Inter-state relations Political horizon of African and international affairs	Creation of UAM and adoption of Charter Creation of UAMD and UAMPT Convention d'Établissement	Presiding: Senghor

5. Bangui	25–27 March 1962	Ahidjo	Houphouet-Boigny, represented by Yacé	UAM and African countries still under colonial rule	Creation of UAM permanent Secretariat at UN in New York	Presiding: Ahidjo
		Dacko				
		Youlou		Possibility of creating common embassy in major capitals		
		Maga	Yameogo, represented by Boudda, Finance Minister		Support of the candidacy of Mauritania for the Security Council	
		Mba		UAM at the UN		
		Tsiranana				
		Ould Daddah		Inter-state relations		
		Hamani Diori				
		Senghor and Dia		UAM and France		
		Tombalbaye				

| Place | Date | Heads of State and Government | | Agenda | Major Decisions | Miscellaneous Observations |
		Present	Absent			
6. Libreville	12–14 September 1962	Ahidjo Dacko Youlou Houphouet-Boigny Maga Mba Yameogo Tsiranana Ould Daddah Hamani Diori Senghor and Dia Tombalbaye	None	UAM and France Congo affair UN agenda Inter-state cooperation	Official rapprochement with Rwanda and Congo-Leopoldville General Convention on technical cooperation concerning personnel among UAM countries Refusal to organize relations between UAM and France—freedom left to states individually	Presiding: Mba Rwanda represented by President Kayibanda Congo-Leopoldville by Bomboko, Foreign Affairs Minister Numerous delegates from revolutionary movements (Angola, Rhodesia, etc.)

Place	Date	Participants		Preparation of Conference at Addis Ababa	Admission of Rwanda to UAM	Presiding: Yameogo
7. Ouagadougou	10–14 March 1963	Ahidjo	Dacko, represented by Macpayen, Foreign Minister			Rwanda represented by Habamenshi, Foreign Minister
		Youlou			Admission of Rwanda to UAM	
		Houphouet-Boigny		Relations between Secretariats	Settlement of Congo-Gabon dispute	
		Maga		Convention of Association with Common Market	Refusal of recognition of Grunitzky government in Togo	
		Mba				
		Yameogo				
		Tsiranana		Broad appraisal of the Togolese question after the assassination of President Sylvanus Olympio	Adoption of motion on necessity of rapid ratification of Convention of Association with Common Market	
		Ould Daddah				
		Hamani Diori				
		Senghor		Inter-state cooperation		
		Tombalbaye			Appointment of new UAM Secretary-General	

[73]

Place	Date	Heads of State and Government		Agenda	Major Decisions	Miscellaneous Observations
		Present	Absent			
8. Cotonou	27–30 July 1963	Ahidjo	Senghor, represented by Diakhate, Information Minister	Draw conclusions from Addis Ababa Conference, where Organization for African Unity (OAU) had been established	Dissolution of the UAM Group and Secretariat at the UN	Yameogo proposed officially dissolution of UAM; Dahomey and Malagasy opposed; question shelved for further study until Dakar Conference
		Maga				
		Yameogo			Admission of Togo	
		Tsiranana	Houphouet-Boigny, represented by Yacé			Yameogo continues as presiding officer
		Ould Daddah				
		Hamani Diori	Kayibanda, represented by Habamenshi			
		Tombalbaye				
		Grunitzky (Togo)	Mba, replaced by Ondo, Foreign Minister			
		Dacko	Youlou, replaced by Vice-President Tchichelle			

Location	Date			Reappraisal of UAM in view of creation of OAU	Suppression of UAM as a political organization	Ould Daddah elected President-in-Office
9. Dakar	7–10 March 1964	Ahidjo	Houphouet-Boigny, represented by Yacé	Reappraisal of UAM in view of creation of OAU	Suppression of UAM as a political organization	Ould Daddah elected President-in-Office
		Apithy (Dahomey)				
		Yameogo	Mba, represented by Anguille, Finance Minister		Creation of UAMCE and appointment of new Secretary-General: Dieng of Senegal	In opposition to Senegal, the Ivory Coast, Niger, and Upper Volta do not sign UAMCE Charter
		Hamani Diori				
		Ould Daddah	Grumitzky, replaced by Amah, Foreign Minister			
		Senghor			All other Secretariats closed, and services integrated in Secretariat of new organization with headquarters in Yaoundé	President Ould Daddah succeeds in calming dispute, calling conference of reconciliation in Nouakchott
		Tsiranana	Kayibanda, not represented			
			Dacko, not represented			
			Massamba-Débat (Congo-Brazzaville), represented by Ockyemba, Minister of Justice			
			Tombalbaye, represented by Ngangtar, Foreign Minister			

Place	Date	Heads of State and Government		Agenda	Major Decisions	Miscellaneous Observations
		Present	Absent			
10. Nouakchott	10–12 February 1965	Ahidjo	Massamba-Débat, represented by Bicoumat, Minister of Interior	Reconcile former UAM partners	Creation of OCAM	Presiding: Ould Daddah
		Ahomadegbé (Dahomey)		Congo affair	Support of Congolese central government (Tshombe)	He seemed to have rallied most of his colleagues to the decisions taken at the Conference
		Yameogo	Kayibanda, not represented	Subversion in Africa		
		Hamani Diori			Ghana accused of being citadel of subversion in Africa	
		Ould Daddah				France officially satisfied at creation of OCAM; declaration by Peyrefitte following Council of Ministers' Meeting, Paris, February 17, 1965
		Senghor				
		Houphouet-Boigny			General de Gaulle invited to visit states of the OCAM	
		Tsiranana				
		Tombalbaye				
		Mba				
		Grunitzky				

11. Abidjan	25–26 May 1965	Houphouet-Boigny Hamani Diori Yameogo Mba Tsiranana Senghor Grunitzky Tombalbaye	Ould Daddah Ahidjo Massamba-Débat Dacko Kayibanda Apithy, represented by Lozes, Foreign Minister	Examine the request for membership of Congo-Leopoldville	In the absence and despite the opposition of several heads of state, including the President-in-office, the Abidjan Conference, called and presided over by Houphouet-Boigny, admitted the Congo-Leopoldville to membership in the OCAM Reaffirmation of accusations against Ghana	The immediate result of the Abidjan Conference was to endanger the existence of the Organization: Mauritania withdrew; Cameroon and Congo-Brazzaville are contemplating withdrawal

E

Excerpts from the Convention
d'Établissement

The Governments of the States of the UAM:

Considering the need to establish in the interest of their nationals on the territory of other States a legal status as close as possible to that of a national, in order to facilitate the exchange and circulation of individuals between States;

Considering that their unanimous desire to affirm solemnly their solidarity and their fraternity implies the conclusion of agreements conferring upon their citizens a status bordering on that of a national;

Have Agreed to Adopt the Following Provisions:

Article 1

The present convention, when ratified, shall apply to the rights and privileges that each of the high contracting parties is disposed to recognize or to accord upon its territory to nationals of the other parties, based upon absolute reciprocity.

Article 2

The citizens of the high contracting parties may freely enter the territory of any of the other parties, travel, establish residence, and freely leave at any time, within the framework of the laws and regulations applicable to nationals—without prejudice to the provisions of police laws and laws of public safety.

Article 3

Under the same conditions and reservations, the nationals of the high contracting parties will enjoy the same rights and liberties as nationals, excepting political rights. The rights and guarantees of the individual set forth by the Universal Declaration of Human Rights will be guaranteed, to wit: the free exercise of cultural, religious, economic, professional, or social activities; individual and civil liberties such as freedom of thought, conscience, religion, worship, opinion, and expression, assembly and association; and the right to organize within the framework of national labor unions.

Article 4

The nationals of each of the high contracting parties may be employed in the Administration of another State under conditions determined by that State's legislation.

Article 8

The Governments of the high contracting parties pledge not to practice any discrimination among their citizens relative to the benefits of access to, and services of, social, cultural, and welfare institutions.

Article 10

Each of the high contracting parties pledges to respect legally acquired rights established on its territory by nationals of the other parties.

Article 13

The citizens of each of the high contracting parties shall enjoy, under the same conditions as nationals, free access to all courts of law to protect and defend their rights.

TANANARIVE, SEPTEMBER 12, 1961

F

Excerpts from the General Convention on the Exchange of Technical Personnel

The Governments of the States of the UAM:

Conscious of the bonds of friendship and solidarity uniting them;

Concerned to manifest a spirit of mutual aid and understanding;

Desiring to assure the functioning of their public services under the best conditions;

In conformity with the Convention d'Établissement signed in Tananarive, with particular reference to Article 4;

Have Agreed upon the Following Provisions:

Article 1

The goal of the present Convention is to define general principles and certain methods of technical cooperation relative to personnel among the States of the UAM.

Article 2

Technical cooperation among the States with respect to personnel may take the following forms:

1. The making available from one State to another of national personnel possessing special qualifications.

2. The training or upgrading of personnel of any State in institutions, educational or administrative, of another State.

Article 3

Each of the signatories pledges to employ the services of the personnel of another State only upon prior agreement of the home State.

Article 4

The Administrative Secretariat of the UAM shall take charge of centralizing the supply and demand for technical cooperation officials and shall bring the same to the attention of the interested parties.

In addition, it shall take charge of centralizing and publicizing the possibilities offered by the States of the UAM for the training and improvement of government personnel, relative to scholarships and openings available to government personnel at institutes, schools, and training centers for public servants and technical personnel.

[80]

Article 17

The technical cooperation officials made available to a State of the UAM, in pursuance of the present Convention, shall exercise their duties under the authority of the Government of that State and shall conform to its rules and regulations.

They shall be bound by the obligation of professional discretion in all matters concerning facts or information devolving from the exercise of their duties.

They shall abstain from any activity adversely affecting the States of the UAM and their Governments.

The States employing such technical cooperation officials shall likewise abstain from requiring of them any activity or demonstration of a character unrelated to their duties.

In the exercise of their duties, the personnel concerned in the present agreement shall generally benefit from the aid and protection of the Government employing them.

Article 20

The States of the UAM pledge themselves to accord priority to the Administrative Secretariat in their requests for personnel made available by the other signatory States.

This provision shall not apply to personnel supplied in pursuance of other special conventions, signed or to be signed outside the framework of the UAM.

In the event that no State shall make an offer within two months of the receipt of a request by the Administrative Secretariat of the UAM, or in the event that the offers presented shall not be accepted by the requesting State, the latter shall retain full freedom of action in recruiting such personnel as it may require.

LIBREVILLE, SEPTEMBER 13, 1962

G

The UAM Stand on African Countries
Still under Colonial Rule

The question of the African countries still under foreign domination was brought up regularly at conferences of the UAM. Frequently, the Administrative Secretariat submitted reports on this subject to the heads of state prior to a conference. Among the most important of these was one presented at Bangui in 1962, reproduced here.

REPORT OF THE UAM SECRETARY-GENERAL ON CONCRETE MEASURES TO ASSIST AFRICAN COUNTRIES NOT YET INDEPENDENT

The principle of aiding African countries not yet independent is accepted by all. The existence on African soil of certain countries still subject to the yoke of colonialism is a challenge to mankind but above all to the independent countries of Africa. It is a threat to the peace of the world and unfavorably affects the evolution of Africa, so true is it that: "Economic and cultural development of young nations cannot take place in a torn and unsettled world."

The fortunate cohesion, the firm determination noticeable in the UAM Group at the UN on the question of Mauritania made possible the admission of the Sister Republic of Mauritania to the world organization. The tireless efforts of various Heads of State of the UAM to mediate between the two parties in the distressing Algerian conflict have finally borne fruit. The question of Mauritania and the Algerian problem demonstrate the fortunate results that a resolute and concerted diplomacy among our twelve can achieve. Now that Mauritania has been admitted to the UN and Algeria is on the threshold of independence, the Heads of State of the UAM must rapidly select other common goals in African foreign policy.

Angola, South Africa, Portuguese Guinea, Spanish Guinea—to cite but a few instances—could constitute targets for our foreign diplomacy. All the Heads of State of the UAM, on different occasions—at international conferences, before the tribune of the UN—have condemned in noble terms the Portuguese repression in Angola, the racism in South Africa, the retrograde policy of Spain in its colonial territories. But what is noteworthy is that this happy unity in the public statements of the most prominent leaders of the UAM has not yet been followed up by concrete proposals. This assistance, which everyone desires and constantly refers to, has remained until now largely theoretical.

We must not settle for lending moral support to our sister countries in the midst of their struggle for national liberation against the colonial powers. If we desire this assistance to have any chance of being effective, demonstrating thereby the reality of the UAM and its African scope, we must give material aid as well.

What form can such assistance take at present, given the precarious state of the finances of most of our States and the inadequacy of our military potential? Precisely in this domain, the States of the UAM can profit from the lessons of the distressing Algerian problem and the various forms of aid furnished by the Arab countries to the GPRA. Assistance might be furnished on four levels: diplomatic, financial, military, and social.

On the Diplomatic Level, assistance might take the form of an unconditional support of subjugated countries at the UN and at various international meetings. The States of the UAM should, in each case, take the initiative in raising the question of decolonization and racism in the course of UN sessions. They should propose punitive measures, such as the expulsion of colonialist or racist powers from international organizations and forbidding South African and Portuguese planes and ships to land on UAM territory.

On the Financial Level, assistance might take the form of a contribution, according to our means, to the different movements for liberation. We can organize or permit the organizing on our territory of collections destined for these movements. Certain performances or even lotteries might be organized and their receipts given entirely to the treasuries of these organizations.

On the Military Level, our States might receive nationals of Angola or South Africa desiring a military training in our armies (at present, this training is often provided in Cairo, Peking, or Moscow). But is this measure truly practical or feasible, given the present conditions of our armies?

On the Intellectual and Social Level, an essential measure is the setting up of centers for welcoming and sheltering refugees. The training of political leaders should also be made a point of honor. Along these lines, the creation of an Institute for the Training of Leaders should be seriously considered. Indeed, the problem of the training of political leaders is crucial for countries striving for independence. The distressing events in the Congo are most certainly the inescapable consequence of the grave insufficiency of trained political leaders. If we desire to avoid the repetition of painful spectacles of that sort in Africa, we must take steps today to prepare Angola and other African countries in the process of achieving independence, by training their future political leaders within our States.

We must face the fact that this is an inescapable duty for us. In addition, this would be an activity within our reach, one with important psychological and political consequences that could only contribute to our advantage internationally. In creating this Institute, we would save our struggling brothers the trek to Peking and Moscow, and we would give an African direction to their liberation movements.

Of course, it is important that the presence on our national territory of refugees or militants from sister states be achieved in the framework of a strict respect for the authority and the institutions of our States. To that end, it would be opportune that a sort of Protocol fix imperatively the rights and duties of the nationals of sister countries struggling against colonialism, to whom we offer our hospitality.

Such measures may seem revolutionary. We believe that they constitute the price that the countries of the UAM must pay in order to help Africa recover its freedom in peace and friendship among its peoples. It has been said, and often repeated, that: "No African country will be truly independent so long as one whit of African territory still remains occupied." Therefore it is the duty of the States of the UAM to participate actively in the decolonization of the African continent.

Now, in numerous regions of Africa, tens of thousands of men and women enamored of freedom continue to fall under the murderous shots of retrograde colonialism. The existence of numerous points of friction represents a grave danger for the areas of Africa already independent. That must not be underestimated. Our continent needs the peace and friendship of its peoples in order to realize its full potential.

There is little doubt that colonial wars are a source of discord and friction between the countries of Europe and the colonized peoples. In addition, it is often rival blocs that confront each other in these wars, through intermediary individuals. The former Belgian Congo is a notorious example. Colonial wars assuredly constitute an open path for the introduction on African soil of forces and ideologies foreign to Africa.

Under these circumstances, no price should be too high to eliminate them, for at the same time we safeguard our character, our cultural integrity, and the original forms of that African civilization that we are so proud today to present to the world.

BANGUI, MARCH 25, 1962

The UAM heads of state held sharply differing views on this question of "decolonization." Great indecision was displayed. Thus the brief resolution on the report submitted at Bangui confined itself to promising "to pursue vigorous and concerted diplomatic action in behalf of the African nationalists . . . ," and the matter was not followed up.

H

The Assassination of President Sylvanus
Olympio

What follows is a narrative written by Gil Olympio, son of the
late Togolese President, in response to a request for a first-hand account of the circumstances surrounding his father's death.

It was 5 P.M., the end of the afternoon of January 12, 1963—a fairly
ordinary afternoon, aside from the Ghanaian ultimatum of the night before—and everything appeared normal. My late father went to his coco-
nut grove in Akodessewa. For the last time.

Toward 8 P.M., he returned. Some friends dropped by. Two and a
half hours later, my parents finished dinner and left the table to retire
for the night. Around 11 P.M., my mother began to hear unusual noises.
When she opened the window, she seemed to make out a group of about
fifty people. She then called my father to have a look. Without further
ado, he assured her, "It must be a group of hooligans or thieves."

Scarcely a half-hour later, my mother heard shots and called my father
again. This time, he could see from the window a battery of machine
guns in front of the house. The shots began to crackle again, flying in
all directions. "Lie flat on your stomach and do what I say," he ordered
my mother. The firing lasted for forty-odd minutes. (The next morning,
January 13, 1963, in the bedroom alone, 400 bullets were counted.) It
must have been around 12:30 when the guns stopped firing. My father,
dressed in short khaki pants, took advantage of the period of calm and
left my mother, telling her, "As soon as you receive word from me, come
join me."

Fifteen minutes later, some ten men, armed with sub-machine guns,
entered. Brandishing their terrifying weapons, they lined up the servants
against the wall and then threatened to shoot my mother if she refused
to reveal where my father was hiding. When they were unable to get
anything out of her, they began to rifle indiscriminately through everything at hand—closets, books, mattresses, and so on.

My mother had about 40,000 francs CFA and 50 Ghanaian pounds in
her wardrobe. They took the money, carried off with them all the liquor
they could find, then shattered the dishes to pieces with bursts of gunfire,
before leaving.

Toward 2 A.M., they again entered my mother's room and threatened her. Being tired, she sat down and told them that she knew nothing of my father's whereabouts. After hesitating several minutes, they went downstairs again. The gunfire began again immediately. About thirty minutes later, they returned for the third time—rather drunk and violent, again threatening to kill my mother. Still unsuccessful after abusing, bullying, and knocking my mother about, they left once more.

It was 5 A.M. My mother was certain of the time, for at just that moment she heard the bells of the Protestant church. Looking out the window, she saw my father seated in an old Buick belonging to Mr. Hussey at the American Embassy. In that instant, she saw four people moving toward the Embassy. They made him get out of the car with his hands raised, and they exchanged several words with him. During this time, two members of the Togolese Unitary Party, Jules Moustapha and Moussa Kona, from Northern Togo, came to see my mother. By their own admission, they came from the military camp, representing Dadjo, who had sent them to tell her that if my father went to the camp and accepted the veterans' claims, there would be no further trouble.

My father then noticed my mother at her window and signaled to her. She went downstairs in her bathrobe, having no time to change, in order to give him the message. As she turned the corner, she heard four shots. When she arrived on the scene, she stood stunned before his lifeless body. A French couple who were our neighbors came to accompany her home.

G. Olympio

Washington, D.C.
June 10, 1965

Books Written under the Center's Auspices

The Soviet Bloc, by Zbigniew K. Brzezinski (jointly with the Russian Research Center), 1960. Harvard University Press.

The Necessity for Choice, by Henry A. Kissinger, 1961. Harper & Bros.

Strategy and Arms Control, by Thomas C. Schelling and Morton H. Halperin, 1961. Twentieth Century Fund.

Rift and Revolt in Hungary, by Ferenc A. Váli, 1961. Harvard University Press.

United States Manufacturing Investment in Brazil, by Lincoln Gordon and Engelbert L. Grommers, 1962. Harvard Business School.

The Economy of Cyprus, by A. J. Meyer, with Simos Vassiliou (jointly with the Center for Middle Eastern Studies), 1962. Harvard University Press.

Entrepreneurs of Lebanon, by Yusif A. Sayigh (jointly with the Center for Middle Eastern Studies), 1962. Harvard University Press.

Communist China 1955-1959: Policy Documents with Analysis, with a Foreword by Robert R. Bowie and John K. Fairbank (jointly with the East Asian Research Center), 1962. Harvard University Press.

In Search of France, by Stanley Hoffmann, Charles P. Kindleberger, Laurence Wylie, Jesse R. Pitts, Jean-Baptiste Duroselle, and François Goguel, 1963. Harvard University Press.

Somali Nationalism, by Saadia Touval, 1963. Harvard University Press.

The Dilemma of Mexico's Development, by Raymond Vernon, 1963. Harvard University Press.

Limited War in the Nuclear Age, by Morton H. Halperin, 1963. John Wiley & Sons.

The Arms Debate, by Robert A. Levine, 1963. Harvard University Press.

Africans on the Land, by Montague Yudelman, 1964. Harvard University Press.

Counterinsurgency Warfare, by David Galula, 1964. Frederick A. Praeger, Inc.

People and Policy in the Middle East, by Max Weston Thornburg, 1964. W. W. Norton & Co.

Shaping the Future, by Robert R. Bowie, 1964. Columbia University Press.

Foreign Aid and Foreign Policy, by Edward S. Mason (jointly with the Council on Foreign Relations), 1964. Harper & Row.

Public Policy and Private Enterprise in Mexico, by M. S. Wionczek, D. H. Shelton, C. P. Blair, and R. Izquierdo, ed. Raymond Vernon, 1964. Harvard University Press.

How Nations Negotiate, by Fred C. Iklé, 1964. Harper & Row.

China and the Bomb, by Morton H. Halperin (jointly with the East Asian Research Center), 1965. Frederick A. Praeger, Inc.

Democracy in Germany, by Fritz Erler (Jodidi Lectures), 1965. Harvard University Press.

The Troubled Partnership, by Henry A. Kissinger (jointly with the Council on Foreign Relations), 1965. McGraw-Hill Book Co.

The Rise of Nationalism in Central Africa, by Robert I. Rotberg, 1965. Harvard University Press.

Communist China and Arms Control, by Morton H. Halperin and Dwight H. Perkins (jointly with the East Asian Research Center), 1965. Frederick A. Praeger, Inc.

Pan-Africanism and East African Integration, by Joseph S. Nye, Jr., 1965. Harvard University Press.

Problems of National Strategy, ed. Henry A. Kissinger, 1965. Frederick A. Praeger, Inc.